THE NEGRO IN NORTHERN BRAZIL

MAP OF THE STATE OF MARANHÁO

MONOGRAPHS OF THE
AMERICAN ETHNOLOGICAL SOCIETY

Edited by MARIAN W. SMITH

XV

OCTAVIO DA COSTA EDUARDO

THE NEGRO IN NORTHERN BRAZIL

A Study in Acculturation

J. J. AUGUSTIN PUBLISHER
NEW YORK

TABLE OF CONTENTS

PREFACE

This study analyzes materials collected during a field trip to the State of Maranhão in northeastern Brazil for a period of nine months from November 1943 to June 1944. Of these nine months, a total of a little more than six weeks were spent in the city of São Luiz, capital of the State. Field work in a rural community in the interior was carried on during two months, and fifteen days were spent in the town of Codó for further observations.

Two special grants from the Rockefeller Foundation to Northwestern University financed the field trip and provided the funds necessary for my spending the academic year 1944-1945 at the University. I am greatly indebted to the Rockefeller Foundation for this financial help, and I also wish to acknowledge my thanks to the Graduate School of Northwestern University for giving me a tuition scholarship. The Rockefeller Foundation further assisted the work by making available funds for publication and I am also grateful for help of the same kind given by the Escolo Livre de Sociologia e Politica de São Paulo.

The field trip to Maranhão was sponsored by the Museu Nacional of Rio de Janeiro, Brazil, a circumstance which was of great advantage to me while in this field. This and other arrangements were made possible through the great kindness of Dona Heloisa Alberto Torres, director of the Musea Nacional, to whom I am deeply grateful.

While in the field many courtesies were extended to me by several persons. I should like here to thank those who were specially helpful in connection with my work: Dr. Francisco Teixeira Leite, Dr. Antonio Lopes, and Senhor and Senhora Tancredo Lago.

Deep gratitude is here expressed to those persons who served as informants and who were so solitious in cooperating for the progress of the research. Without their kind cooperation the work could not have been carried on. I am truly grateful to them both for professional reasons and for having received their trust and liking, and I shall always remember Mãe Andreza, Dudú, Maneco, José, Siqueira, Djalma, Dona Maria, Victor, and Seu Valério among many others with the affectionate remembrance expressed so well by the Portuguese word *saudade*.

vii

Dr. Richard A. Waterman and Mr. Alfred Rockefeller, Jr., gave generously of their time to editing parts of the manuscript and offered many valuable suggestions. I wish to express my sincere thanks to them and to Miss Catherine Weaver who translated into English the chapter on the family and the section on magic which were originally written in Portuguese.

I obtained my training in anthropology under the direction of Dr. Melville J. Herskovits and the field work in Brazil was also directed by him. This dissertation was written under his guidance. For his aid, inspiration and encouragement I shall always be profoundly grateful.

CHAPTER ONE

Processes of Acculturation

The systematic study of contact between peoples having different cultures is one of the principal concerns of modern anthropology. This is a recent development, for not until 1936 did anthropologists discuss at length the problems to be considered and the orientations to be followed in this new field of studies. At that time, acculturation, as the studies of cultural contact followed by borrowing are called, was defined by a Sub-Committee of the Social Science Research Council as "those phenomena which result when groups of individuals having different cultures come into continuous first-hand contact, with subsequent changes in the original cultural pattern of either or both groups."[1]

Among the problems on which light can satisfactorily be thrown through studies of acculturation are those which concern cultural stability or instability. When peoples of different cultures are in sustained contact the rate of resistance to change in different cultural aspects and the factors which contribute to the preservation of elements of culture or to their change can best be observed. Such study is naturally complemented by the consideration of what has been incorporated by each group into its earlier way of life and of the manner in which this has been achieved. This is a dynamic approach, the interest of which centers not only on the results of cultural contact but equally on the processes by means of which traditions with which a people have come into contact are taken over and earlier traditions are maintained, modified or lost. It is important whether what is preserved and what is taken over form an integrated whole or not, and the factors behind the process of integration or non-integration also constitute an important problem.

The questions just raised will be discussed in the present work with reference to the Negroes of a rural and an urban community in the State of Maranhão in the northeastern part of Brazil who, to varying degrees, have been exposed to European ways of life. The following are the points with which the present investigation will be concerned; the preservation

[1] Redfield, Linton and Herskovits, 1936.

1

of African ways of life, the acceptance of European customs and institutions, the degrees of integration which have been achieved between African and European traditions to form the present culture of the Maranhão Negroes, and the conditions and processes which have worked to make this culture what it is today. Answers to these questions should make some contribution to our knowledge of what happens to African cultures in contact and to the wider problems of cultural dynamics, either confirming, modifying or denying assumptions or conclusions which have been reached concerning these specialized and general fields of study.

Some concepts and tools for research and interpretation of materials which have been devised in these fields will be tested in the present work. They are, especially, the concept of cultural focus and the concept of the Old World cultural province. A cultural focus is that aspect of a people's culture which is more stressed than any other, and around which the lives of the people center. This phenomena "points a significant mechanism operative in inducing and encouraging, but also in regulating, cultural change."[2] As studies of Negro cultures in the New World have thus far shown, the focal point of a culture seems to be its most persistent aspect, which in psychological terms implies that not all life values are as meaningful nor as highly regarded as others, and that people cling more tenaciously to those values which are more important to them. Hence these more important life values, which are obviously culturally determined, are less subject to change than others having less moment. This concept has simplified the understanding of why Negroes in parts of the New World have preserved religious survivals and orientations more carefully than economic, social or artistic aspects of African culture. Here we ask whether or not this mechanism is also operative among the Maranhão Negro groups.

The concept of an Old World cultural province[3] is based on similarities in folklore, religion, and other aspects of the cultures of the peoples of Europe, Africa and southern Asia. Though the autonomy of European, Asiatic and African civilizations is obvious, it must at the same time be recognized that they share similar traditions and institutions. This is an important point for the study of Negro cultures in the New World, for if Europeans and Africans have certain cultural orientations that resemble each other it can be assumed that when these African and European cultural aspects are brought into contact they may reinforce each other or even merge into a single whole. This merging of religious and other

[2] Herskovits, 1945, p. 168.
[3] Herskovits, 1941, p. 18.

cultural forms has received the name of syncretization, most widely recognized in the field of religion and something to which the Maranhão Negroes are no exception.

This paper will consider not only the degree of amalgamation between African and European beliefs and practices in the two communities, however, but also the process by which this has been achieved. Attention, both in the field work and in the presentation of the material, centered upon the general problem of African survivals among the Negroes of northern Brazil. Indian survivals in today's population present another acculturative problem which has been touched on here only slightly.[4]

Similarity of cultural patterns such as those of Africa and Europe may not lead to amalgamation, but may instead facilitate the acceptance of foreign traditions when one of the groups is in a subordinate position, as in the case of the Negroes in the Americas. Whether either the merging or the re-interpretation so evident in the field of religion, obtains in such other fields as economic life and family structure is a question which the present study will also attempt to answer.

It is to be stressed that all these problems—the preservation of African traditions, the adoption of those of European origin and the degree of merging in both—in Maranhão or in the other localities, can only be studied from a dynamic point of view, if we are to gain an understanding or more than the institutional aspects of acculturation. This implies that the actual factors involved in the acculturative process are the reactions of the individuals concerned in the situation of contact, whether this involves their adopting new customs or maintaining those they had previously, should all be investigated. Only in this way can we learn something of the socio-psychological mechanisms directly involved in the acculturative process.[5] To round out our understanding, furthermore, it is also essential to follow the acculturative process as it develops through short and long periods of time.

As has been indicated, the approach which has been outlined thus far will be applied to the study of the Negro cultures of two communities in Maranhão with consideration given to the discussion of problems of cultural conservatism, change, and integration. Since the research on which the present work is based has been carried on in a rural and in an urban community, we have the advantage of being able to investigate the acculturative processes in two different settings, and to compare the results

[4] See Wagley, n. d.
[5] Hallowell, 1945, pp. 171-200.

achieved in each. Has the urban environment facilitated acculturation more than the rural setting? Is the urban group more European and less African than the rural? What have been and what are the factors at work in both communities? Has integration of religious beliefs and other cultural forms, if this has been achieved at all, been greater in the interior than in the city? Why? These are all problems which this work will seek to answer.

CHAPTER TWO

Two Communities of Maranhao

Negro slavery in the State of Maranhão was concentrated in two places: in São Luiz, the capital, and in the southwestern part of the state that to-day comprises the municipalities of Caxias and Codó.

In the nineteenth century, large cotton and rice plantations in this region were worked by slave labor. But with the abolition of slavery in 1888 these large holdings of land, then in decline, were completely liquidated. The white landowners either sold their lands to their former slaves and departed, or simply abandoned them. In a few instances they gave the lands to their former slaves. Meanwhile the ex-servants, except for the rather large group that migrated to the cities of São Luiz and Caxias and to the town of Codó, remained on the lands they had formerly worked, those who had slaves thus becoming owners by right of title or of occupation. There was so much land that the problem of making a division and marking off a plot for each did not arise. The plantations were broken up and in their place appeared small rural communities situated a few kilometers from each other: communities which today are inhabited chiefly by the descendants of the ex-slaves on the former plantations.

Santo Antônio dos Pretos, one of these communities, is located in the municipality of Codó, sixty kilometers from the town of the same name. As in other settlements, most of its population of 150 have descended from former slaves who lived here or nearby, though a few of them are old people who themselves knew slavery. Those of its inhabitants who have come from nearby regions do not differ from persons born in Santo Antônio in ethnic origin or in cultural patterns. The only other elements in the population there consist of a white family of three and a small group of persons who have migrated from the neighboring State of Piauí. The latter are a mixture of Indian, White and Negro stocks, who have already been or are now being assimilated into this rural society. The newcomers have the same rural background and many of the religious traditions and attitudes which characterize the rural Negro of Maranhão, so that no difficulties stand in the way of their assimilation. Thus, with the exceptions indicated,

5

the Negro group of Santo Antônio is characterized by ethnic homogeneity, preserved during and after slavery.

Only two of the Negroes in this community are literate. Of these two, one is an old man, a former slave, the other a man thirty years old. Three sons of one inhabitant are students in the primary school in the town of Codó, where they are being trained for trades as well as learning reading and writing. This, however, is not common. In the main, the young people in Santo Antônio, as their parents before them, do not receive any formal education.

In contrast to Santo Antônio, with its markedly homogeneous population, the urban Negroes constitute a heterogeneous group, both from the ethnic and the cultural point of view. Ethnic heterogeneity came about because of the degree of crossing among Negroes, Whites, and persons of mixed Indian-White and Indian-Negro descent who came from the interior of Maranhão. The groups studied in this work, however, are of pure or predominantly African descent, to whom the term Negro is applied in accordance with Brazilian usage, in which sense it will be used here. Census data are lacking on the color distribution of the city's population, so that it is not possible to do other than approximate the numerical strength of the Negro physical type in São Luiz. However, a conservative estimate would be that thirty per cent of the city's 60,000 people, i.e about 20,000 persons, are of pure or predominately African descent. Although the total life of the Negroes in São Luiz was taken into account and served as a background for the detailed study of the groups whose members could be identified as carriers of African traditions, only a small portion of these 20,000 persons could be studied, since the main purpose of this research was to study groups who still preserve African cultural survivals.

In contrast to the rural Negroes, the Negroes of São Luiz have had continuous contact with white fellow-citizens whose behavior patterns and attitudes differ from theirs in various aspects. These differences are found in certain economic aspects of life, in the ways of establishing a family, in religious and magical beliefs, and in moral patterns. The urban Negroes are, of course, aware of these differences, but so are the rural Negroes, who are only in slight contact with the Whites of the town of Codó, where similar patterns to those of São Luiz white society are found. The principal differences here between the reaction of the two groups is that cultural patterns of the White figure as much more important factors in the lives of the urban Negroes who are, in turn, much more highly sensitized to them.

In the country, all the Negroes earn their living by working in the fields;

in the city, members of the more heterogeneous Negro community follow various occupations. In the village, all are Roman Catholics and all attend ritual dances of African origin, either to take an active part or simply as observers, all in general sharing the same attitudes, the same beliefs and the same points of view. In the city, however, there are Negroes who do not belong to the Catholic Church, but to the Protestant or Spiritualist churches. Only a minority of these Negroes participate in the ceremonies of African derivation which are held in cult houses. However, many who profess to be Catholics take part in these ceremonies, while in addition to beliefs of African and European origin, Indian beliefs and practices are found, making the acculturative situation more complex.

TABLE I

Tribal Origins of Slave Population

Provenience	São Luiz *Inventários*									Códo *Inventários*		Total
	1800	1815	1820	1829	1837	1841	1847	1855	1860	1838	1847	
Creole	57	55	29	55	41	19	109	154	14	16	5	554
ANGOLO-CONGO												
Angolá	19	44	8	15	5	6	8	5	3	1	1	115
Benguela		6	3	5	1	4		3				22
Cabinda			4	4	4			4		2		18
Casange		1		2	1	1		2				7
Angico		1			2	3				2		8
Congo	1		3	2	2	2		2		5		17
Total												187
SENEGAL												
Mandinga	14	13	6	9	1	2	9		1			55
Cacheo	20	12	2	1	3	1				1		40
Bijago	14	7	1	1			2			1		26
Balanta	4	1			2					1		8
Felup	1								2			3
Cabo Verde					3							3
Bambara					2							2
Nalu								1				1
Ciafa		1										1
Total												139
GUINEA COAST												
Mina	3	27	1	3	3	1		1	1	2	1	43
Nago			1	4								5
Calabar			1									1
Total												49
Mozambique		3		4	1	1				1		10
Camunda	1								1			2
Africans								30	40			70
Total	134	171	54	102	68	51	128	202	62	32	7	1011

Slave origins and cultural traditions. The Negroes of Maranhão come from different regions of Africa. According to the information contained in about 100 *inventários*[1] consulted in São Luiz and in the town of Codó they came principally from four regions: what is today the Portuguese colony of Angola, from the neighboring Congo regions, from the Guinea Coast, and from Senegal in the region of the present colony of Portuguese Guinea. In Table I, slaves who had different owners are classified according to their common tribal origin[2] (with the exception of the creole slaves, who were born in Brazil) and according to the years in which the *inventários* were made.

As is to be seen, the Angola contribution, which includes the Negroes termed Angolas, Benguelas and Casanges, was considerable. This is especially true if to their number are added the Cabindas, the Cacongo and other related tribes from the region near the coast and directly north of the Congo River, and the Angicos, also known as the Bateke, who were introduced in small numbers from the region adjacent to this river but at some distance from the coast. Table I indicates that the Negroes who came to Maranhão from the Senegal were principally Mandingas and Cacheos, the latter lived near the Cacheo River. Slaves named Bijagos (from the Bijago or Bisago Islands near the mainland), Cabo Verde, Felupes, Bambara and Nalus were much less numerous. It is also to be noted that, according to announcements published in the newspaper *O Publicador Maranhense* on August 19, 1854, Fula Negroes, or Peuhls, as they are called by the French, were also to be found in Maranhão. In addition to slaves from Angola, the Congo and Senegal, we find that "Mina," Yoruban (Nago), Camunda, and Mozambique Negroes were also introduced into Maranhão. Mozambique slaves, apparently few in number, were shipped from the area now comprised by the colony of that name on the southeastern coast of Africa. It was not possible to determine the origin of the Camunda slaves, but this is unimportant, since only a few seem to have been imported into Maranhão. Calabar slaves, who came also in small numbers, derive from the Calabar

[1] The *inventário* is an official inventory, made upon the death of a person, for the purpose of validating the inheritance of his holdings. During slavery, it listed slaves as well as other types of property.

[2] Information on the classification of African tribes according to geographical areas is found in accessible form in Delafosse, 1931. As given here, the provenience of the Negro groups who were brought into Maranhão is in accord with the findings of Dr. G. A. Beltran, who has ascertained with great care the origin of Negro slaves introduced into Mexico. His data, which are valid for all of the New World, will appear in his forthcoming book on the history of the Negroes in Mexico.

region of the Guinea Coast, i. e. the district which includes the mouths of the Niger River.

The relatively high percentage of "Mina" slaves, especially in the year 1815, supposed to be Negroes from the Gold Coast, raises an interesting and important question. Does it indicate that Negroes from this region entered Maranhão in great numerical strength? The answer to this question remains somewhat uncertain since it is still possible that the term as used in Brazil signified Africans from a much wider region than the Gold Coast.[3] There is reason to believe that "Mina Coast" was used in Brazil to refer to the entire Guinea Coast. Nina Rodrigues, who at the end of the nineteenth century made the first studies of African religions in Brazil, suggests that Minas were slaves from the Gold Coast, Ivory Coast and Slave Coast, the latter including Togoland, Dahomey and western Nigeria: "É provavel que na denominação generica de Minas se comprehendessem no Rio de Janeiro onde dominavam os Bantús, todos pos povos da Costa do Marfim, do Ouro e dos Escravos."[4] He based his assumption on the list of Negroes made by the French painter Debret who lived in Rio de Janeiro in the beginning of the nineteenth century. Some groups of slaves found in the city at that time were: "Minas, Minas-Negos, Minas Mahys and Minas Cavallos."[5] The *Regimento dos Officiaes da Alfandega* (Customs Registry) of Bahia for September 27, 1771, states that the slaves brought to Brazil were from two regions: the "Mina Coast" and Angola.[6] No mention is made of other regions, and yet Yoruban and Dahomean groups are most often mentioned in the literature as the most numerous.[7] From 1785 to 1795, only 29,172 slaves from the Mina Coast were brought to Bahia. But over 47,000 "Minas" and 11,000 Angolas were brought in from 1797 to 1806.[8] As no mention is made of the many Dahomean and Yoruban slaves who were introduced into Bahia, the student is led to conclude that slaves from these regions were included in the term "Minas." In support of this position, it should be mentioned that old informants in São Luiz referred to Africans whom

[3] Ramos (1943, Vol. I, p. 352) shares this opinion.
[4] Rodrigues, 1932, pp. 164-165.
[5] The second designations refer to tribes from the Guinea Coast. Nago refers to the Yoruban people, Mahys to the Dahomeans. The designation Cavallos is perhaps connected with the region of the Cavally River which separates Liberia from the Ivory Coast.
[6] Amaral, 1927, p. 454.
[7] *Ibid.*, pp. 474, 477; Rodrigues, 1932, pp. 159, 162; Ramos, 1943, Vol. I, pp. 352-353, 390.
[8] Calogeras, 1938, pp. 322, 325-326.

they had known or heard of as "Minas-Nagos, Minas-Geges, Minas-Fulupas, and even Minas-Angolas and Minas-Cambindas," among other terms. It must also be noted that nowhere in Brazil are Gold Coast survivals to be found.[9]

African cultural retentions in Maranhão which can be traced with certainty derive from Angolan, Yoruban and Dahomean peoples. But Yoruban slaves are barely mentioned in the *inventários* that were analyzed, and no mention at all is made of those from Dahomey. What is the explanation? Perhaps, as suggested above, they were introduced under the general term "Mina"; this is supported by the fact that the descendents of Dahomean slaves in São Luiz, easily identified because they have preserved a great many Dahomean religious traditions, call themselves simply "Minas" or "Minas-Geges," Gege being the term used by Brazilian Negroes for those of Dahomean origin. There is thus no doubt that Dahomean slaves were introduced into São Luiz, though apparently in small numbers, while it is also certain that some of them were taken to the rural areas. The village studied, for instance, has little or no contact with São Luiz, yet Dahomean survivals are found there. The matter is of considerable significance, for though Yoruban and Dahomean Negroes were introduced in small numbers, it will be seen that their influence on the Maranhão Negroes has been great.

This knowledge of the tribal origins of the Africans brought to Maranhão is particularly important in a study such as this because it provides the means whereby a cultural base line, indispensable in a study of acculturation and cultural change, can be established. We have seen that slaves were brought into Maranhão from four regions of Africa: Angola, Congo, Senegal, and the Guinea Coast. The cultures of the tribes in each one of these areas are alike in many respects. Modes of life, beliefs and social institutions are similar enough so that they can be compared with each other, despite the fact that the tribes are three different African cultural areas.[10] Thus, Negroes from Angola who were introduced into Maranhão as well as those from the Congo, are from the Congo area; Dahomeans and Yorubas are from the Guinea Coast area; and Senegal is located in the Western Sudanese area. There are, however, striking resemblances between the cultures of the areas of Africa, especially between those just named, when these are contrasted, as a whole, to European and American Indian cultures. Thus, peoples living far apart in Africa had similar cultural orientations, and their cultures had enough common denominators, to make it possible to set up our base line without too great difficulty.

[9] Ramos, 1940, p. 56.
[10] Herskovits, 1941, pp. 77-85.

We may now turn to a discussion of some items in which these African cultures show similarities pertinent to this study. The discussion need not be comprehensive, since certain aspects of the African cultural heritage have been lost by Maranhão Negroes; and it will not be necessary to discuss the intricacies of African sib organization, the mechanics of political control, the system of divining and the tradition of the graphic arts, since none of these are found in Maranhão. African patterns of economic life, family organization and religion will be of primary concern.

The Negroes who came to Maranhão gained their subsistence from agriculture. In the Congo and in Angola, women cultivate the soil.[11] Among the Yorubu and Dahomeans, men clear the fields, but women cultivate them and sell the produce and other goods in the markets, often keeping their profits for themselves and thus enjoying a great deal of economic independence.[12] Women in the Congo and Angola also seem to have the same high economic status as the Yoruban and Dahomean women. Thus, "each Ovimbundu girl," says Hambly,[13] "cultivates a small patch of ground, the produce of which she is at liberty to sell in order to buy brass ornaments, beads, and palm oil." Weeks points out that "women loom large in Congo village and town life . . ."[14] adding to this that "the free woman of ordinary intelligence, of average skill in farming and cooking has in all things that pertain to women pretty much her own way."[15]

Economic life in the Guinea Coast shows a high degree of complexity in its organization, and in its distributional processes. In addition to this, patterns of discipline and hierarchy mark the productive cycle, expressing themselves through patterns of cooperative labor in agriculture. Both the Yorubu and the Dahomeans have large cooperative groups to work the fields, called *owe* by the Yorubu and *dokpwe* by the Dahomeans.[16] Cooperation also seems to mark productive activities in the Congo.[17] In Senegal, among the Peuhle (Fula) of the Fouta-Djallon region, large cooperative groups are likewise employed to prepare the land and harvesting is sometimes done cooperatively.[18]

[11] Weeks, 1914, p. 103; Hambly, 1914, p. 146.
[12] Herskovits, 1938, Vol. I, pp. 35, 56, 86.
[13] Hambly, 1914, p. 146.
[14] Weeks, 1914, p. 105.
[15] *Ibid*, p. 106.
[16] Bascom, 1941, p. 44; Herskovits, 1938, Vol. I, p. 63.
[17] Weeks, 1914, p. 103.
[18] Tauxier, 1937, p. 377. This writer quotes Paul Guebhard, *Au Fouta-Dialon*, p. 52.

Family organization[19] in the areas from which the Brazilian slaves were drawn follows a polygynous pattern, descent in the main being counted on the father's side. Other relationship groups are the extended family and the sib, kinship groups which have disappeared entirely among the Brazilian Negroes of Maranhão. The membership of the sib groups is composed both of the living and of the dead, for the ancestors invariably play an important role in them. As supernatural members of the sib, of importance among other supernatural beings, they may help their living descendants or punish them in accordance with the service rendered them. This gives rise to a cult of the ancestors which expresses itself by elaborate mortuary ceremonies and offerings to the dead and which is fundamental in the culture of these Negro tribes.

The cult of the ancestors is only one of the aspects shared in common by the religions of the peoples in Senegal, the Guinea Coast and Congo.[20] Other aspects have to do with beliefs in nature deities, in multiple souls and in magic powers. In all these areas, the supernatural is an integral part of the daily life of the people, and is thus of immediate importance to all human beings. The Yoruban and Dahomean worship of anthropomorphic deities by means of elaborate rituals is carried on by religious organizations with priests and initiates. Dances are held to honor these deities, who on such occasions "possess" the cult initiates. The songs and drum-rhythms that accompany such dances are important in the ceremonies. The worship of nature deities seems to follow the same pattern in Senegal; thus, the religious societies described by Tauxier in his book on the Bambara seem to be like the Dahomean and Yoruban cult groups.

Since the peoples of Senegal, the Guinea Coast, the Congo and Angola share common cultural orientations, slaves brought to Maranhão can be considered to have had similar cultural endowments, a point which is important to establish before entering the discussion of Negro acculturation in Maranhão. For through the common denominators of their cultures, patterns of behavior and of belief were shared by persons from different

[19] For a discussion of the family among the Fula, see Tauxier's (1937) resumé of Guebhard's discussion, pp. 374-376; for a study of the family in Dahomey see Herskovits, 1938. Weeks, (1914) discusses family in the Congo, and Hambly (1914) discusses Angola's family's arrangements for the Ovimbundu.

[20] Books on which this outline of African religions is based are: Tauxier, 1927 and 1937, for the Senegal; Herskovits, 1938, for the Dahomeans; Johnson, 1921, and Farrow, 1926, for the Yoruba; Weeks, 1914, for the Congo; Pechuel-Loesche, 1907, and Hambly, 1914, for Angola.

provinces and could thus in this New World setting be transmitted to their descendants as a unified and integrated body of custom.

African slaves were brought to Maranhão only after 1761, more than two centuries after the introduction of Negro slaves into other parts of Brazil. It was at this time that the Indians, who had until then been enslaved, were supplanted by Negroes. How many slaves came in directly from Africa or were brought in through the inland route from Bahia is not known, but there is little doubt that the forced migration of Negroes to the State of Maranhão was quite large. In 1873, according to Gayozo, who studied life in Maranhão at the beginning of the nineteenth century, this region received 1545 slaves.[21] Martius, the German naturalist and traveller, estimated that 3,500 Negroes were imported in Maranhão annually in the first years of the same century.[22] Cesar Marques, a historian born in São Luiz, states that 30,356 slaves were introduced in his home state from 1812 to 1820,[23] while Roberto Simonsen, in his study of the economic history of Brazil, gives 45,777 as the number of Negroes imported during the period from 1812 to 1821.[24] In 1819, there were 133,332 slaves and only 66,668 free persons in Maranhão.[25] These figures show clearly that the slave traffic to the State of Maranhão was of very considerable proportions until 1821, at least; and though no data are available for the period that follows until the year 1853, it is fair to assume that the traffic continued in some strength after 1821. This assumption is based on the fact that the period of economic prosperity which began in Maranhão at the end of the eighteenth century continued for four or five decades, until after the twenties of the nineteenth century.[26] Due to this fact the need for slaves on the plantations, as well as for domestic service and to hire out in São Luiz, remained constant.

At the end of the nineteenth century, there were but few persons of African birth in Maranhão. In a trip made to São Luiz in 1896, Nina Rodrigues found only two old African women: both of whom said they were from the Guinea Coast of Africa.[27] Today, only a few Negroes who live in

[21] Prado Junior, 1942, p. 147. Information derived from the *Compendio historico politico dos principios da lavoura* Souza Gayozo, Paris, 1818.

[22] *Ibid.*

[23] Marques, 1870, p. 200.

[24] Simonsen, 1937, Vol. II, p. 168.

[25] Calogeras, 1938, p. 330. These figures are given by the Conselheiro Leão Velloso.

[26] Simonsen, 1937, p. 169.

[27] Rodrigues, 1932.

this city still know the tribal origins of their ancestors, in most cases these
having been Yoruban and, even more frequently, Dahomean. In the rural
districts studied, however, not even the word Africa is heard. There was one
old man, now in his seventies, who remembered the name "Bijago" and
mentioned the term *"contrabanda"* which is also used in the city to designate Africans brought to Maranhão. It should be pointed out here, however,
that at least some generations separate the living rural Negroes from their
African ancestors, something not quite so true of some groups of city dwellers. In an *inventário* made in Codó in 1847, for instance, of nine slaves
mentioned only two were Africans, an Angola and a "Mina," forty-five and
fifty years old respectively. In another *inventário* made in 1866, only one
slave of twenty-five had been born in Africa. This person, eighty-four years
old, was from Angola. In an *inventário* made in 1869, all the slaves mentioned were of Brazilian birth.

Most São Luiz Negroes are likewise separated from Africa by some generations, as shown by the *inventários* that were analyzed. Nevertheless, the
fact that some people know the tribal derivation of their ancestors leads
one to think that Africans may have been introduced into São Luiz after
the importation of slaves to the interior had been stopped. Evidence for
this assumption is, however, precarious. In two *inventários* made in 1867
in São Luiz, only two African slaves were counted among more than thirty.
The two African women whom Nina Rodrigues found in São Luiz in 1896
were very old and in this connection, it is significant to note that the only
two groups of city Negroes who trace their descent to specific tribes of
Africa state that they are of the same Yoruban and Dahomean peoples to
which the old ladies said they belonged.

If we reverse our emphasis, and attempt to discover the earliest dates of
arrival for one or both of these tribes, we encounter certain facts concerning
the group of Dahomean descent that should be mentioned here. As will be
seen later, this group is familiar with the name of the Dahomean king Agongolo or Agongoro, who ruled over Dahomey from 1789 to 1797 according to
Le Herissé, and from 1789 to 1818 according to Burton and Skertchly.[28]
This name slightly modified to Agongono, with the accent on the penulti-
mate syllable instead of the ante-penult as pronounced in Dahomey, is
given to one of the deities worshipped by the group, and may be taken to
indicate that Dahomean slaves came to Maranhão in the late eighteenth or
the early nineteenth century. This does not mean that Dahomean slaves
were not brought later, but it is rather intriguing to discover that the name

[28] Herskovits, 1938, Vol. I, p. 13.

of the great king Chezo who reigned from 1818 to 1858 is entirely unknown
to these people. This suggests that the proportion of slaves introduced before 1818 was greater than that introduced after 1818. In this connection,
we can note again that most "Mina" slaves were mentioned in the *inventários* for the year 1815. For a definite conclusion we need more detailed
data, but the materials just discussed are suggestive. If later data confirm
what these materials indicate, the Dahomean group may be said to have
maintained its identity in Maranhão for a period of over 150 years.

Negro slaves were employed on the large cotton plantations in the
interior of the state, especially in the region of Caxias, where more than
half of the cotton grown in Maranhão was obtained.[29] Gayozo observed
in 1818 that an average plantation employed fifty slaves,[30] which means
that some estates had a much larger number. This is borne out by the
inventários, which show that many families owned 20, 30, 40, 50 and even
more slaves. But when Maranhão economic life, based on slavery and on
cotton, suffered reverses after the second half of the nineteenth century, a
great many of these slaves were sold to owners in the southern part of Brazil,
especially in Rio de Janeiro. From 1860 to 1869, 3,600 slaves were ex-
ported from Maranhão, says Cesar Marques.[31] Newspapers of this period
published daily requests from slave owners to the authorities to embark
slaves to Rio. Urban as well as rural Negroes were shipped, the migration
of the rural slaves being recalled even today in the words of a song sung
during African religious dances in Santo Antônio and other neighboring
communities:

Santa Bárbara,	St. Barbara,
Eu fui vendido	I've been sold
Pro Rio de Janeiro	To go to Rio de Janeiro
Pro Rio de Janeiro	To go to Rio de Janeiro
Não chora, mamãe,	Don't cry, mother
Não chora.	Don't cry.

What is known concerning the acculturative situation of the Negroes in
Maranhão? What opportunities did the Africans have to preserve their
traditions and transmit them to their offspring and these, in their turn, to
theirs? What factors in the situation in which they found themselves facilitated or hindered the preservation of the African cultural heritage?

It must be noted, first of all, that in accordance with the *inventários*
slaves from different tribes and different regions lived together both on the

[29] Melo Franco, 1944, p. 119.
[30] Quoted by Prado, 1942, p. 147.
[31] Marques, 1870, p. 200.

plantations and in the city. In one *inventário* dated 1838, the town of Codó, the following slaves are mentioned: sixteen creoles (born in Brazil), two "Minas," two Cabindas, one Balanta, one Bijago, two Angicos, five Congo, one Cacheo, one Angola and one Mozambique. A São Luiz *inventário* of 1820 names nine slaves as creoles, two Mandinga, two Angolas, one Congo, one "Mina" and one Benguela, one Felupe, one Nalu, two Cabindas and one Casange.

The fact that slaves from different parts of Africa were thrown together in the New World has been interpreted by some authors as an impediment to the preservation of African traditions.[32] This theory, however, does not take into consideration the common cultural orientations of Africans brought to the New World. Finding themselves in identical situations, they thus adapted themselves to them, or interpreted the situations in a similar manner. Just which of these common orientations, which specific tribal traits were preserved in this way by the African slaves introduced into Maranhão and transmitted to their descendants will be seen in the chapters that follow. For the present, we are concerned with analyzing the rural and urban situation in which the slaves found themselves. As indicated, the provenience of Africans in São Luiz and Santo Antônio was the same, i.e., both regions received slaves from all regions that have been mentioned, and in similar proportion.

Conditions of slavery. On the large plantations, most of the slaves worked in the fields; a smaller number were employed in domestic service. Both men and women cultivated the fields, the latter being spared only the work of clearing the bush. The work day began at four o'clock in the morning, when a bell was struck and the overseers knocked at the houses of the slaves to be sure they awakened. Not before five o'clock in the afternoon did the slaves finish with their work. They reached the seat of the plantation between six and seven o'clock at night, still having to prepare a large portion of rice by pounding it in the mortars. It was only after this that they could go to their cabins for the evening meal.[33]

In the city, the slaves were employed either like those in domestic service on the plantations or, in accordance with what is stated in the *inventários*, as bakers, carpenters, confectioners, tailors, and masons. They were also called on to perform various kinds of unskilled labor. Thus one of the *inventários* states that money is owed to a certain person because he rented

[32] Reuter, 1938, p. 199.
[33] This description of the slave's daily life was given by an old man who had himself been a slave in his youth.

two Negroes and one Negro woman for a period of ninety-two days.[34] It is seen that slaves of both sexes were in this category of *"excravos de service,"* rented slaves. By renting them their owners received a large margin of profit.[35] Domestic slaves, who worked in the homes of their owners, were also numerous in São Luiz not only because they were needed to care for the house but also because to have many slaves gave the owner prestige.[36]

Whatever the occupational differentation between domestic slaves and those dedicated to other purposes, the former were in closer contact with their white owners than the latter. This does not necessarily signify, however, that they were more influenced by European tradition. Domestic slaves shared their experiences with the others when they all came together at night in the slave quarters on the plantations, or in the basements of the city mansions. Yet all slaves were exposed to cultural patterns of the whites and some were even taught to read and write. This does not seem, however, to have greatly changed their mode of thinking, or their basic attitudes and conceptions of the universe: at the present time one finds that literate Negroes, whether in the rural community or in the city, are similar in these respects to Negroes without schooling.

Both historical documents and oral traditions, still alive in the city, testify that Maranhão slaves were badly, and even cruelly treated. Most commonly recalled by Negroes and Whites alike are stories in which female slaves were victims of a jealous sadism of their white mistresses. Though in other parts of Brazil, where the patriarchal system predominated, the slaves are said to have been treated more humanely,[37] in Maranhão the slaves were introduced too late to permit the establishment and consolidation of this system. It is to this absence that the historian Caio Prado attributes the severe treatment of slaves in the region with which we are concerned.[38] What influence these cruelties may have exercised on the preservation or loss of the African traditions cannot be evaluated with any degree of validity, because of the lack of data on specific acculturative

[34] Por alluguel dos pretos Antonio e Ignacio nos meses de 7bro, 8bro, 9bro e dezbro 92 dias uteis a 320 rs.
58$889 e idem da mulata Luiza nos meses indicados a 200 rs. sendo 92 dias uteis 18$400.
[35] "um ramo particular de negócio," says Prado (1942, p. 220) about the renting of slaves in Brazil.
[36] "intervem a par das legítimas necessidades do serviço doméstico, a vaidade dos senhores que se alimenta com números avultados de servos." *Ibid,* p. 276.
[37] *Ibid.;* Pierson, 1942, Chap. III.
[38] Prado, 1942, p. 276.

situations. But this element in the life of the Negroes must at least be mentioned to fill in any account of their background.

The majority of the Negroes in this region seem to have accepted their slave status without serious protest; but there were many who did not tolerate slavery, and made efforts to become free. Runaway slaves were as common in Maranhão as in other parts of Brazil in the nineteenth century, and São Luiz newspapers frequently published advertisements asking for the return of these runaways. Thus *O Publicador Maranhense* in its number of May 5, 1854, publishes four of these announcements. In its issue of June 8 of the same year it advertises that two slaves, "one creole" and the other "of the color of Fula people" had escaped from the São Paula plantation in the Pindare valley; the same issue carries the news that a male slave who ran away had been apprehended, while a female slave had also been taken into custody for being out too late without her owner's license.[39] The same journal, in its number of June 13, also stated that a female runaway slave had been recaptured,[40] and on August 19 it states that two Negroes "of the black Fula nation" had run away.

Case after case testifies the unwillingness of slaves in both city and country to accept slavery. In Santo Antônio, the people still speak of the *mocambos*, localities where escaped slaves were wont to hide. One old man, who had been a slave, tells how several times he escaped from his owners and went to a *mocambo* where he hid until he thought his master had forgotten about the incident. Such tales, whatever their historical exactitude, do indicate that slavery was not tolerated by all Negroes; and it is not unreasonable to assume that a much larger number would have escaped had they had the opportunity. However, no series of revolts occurred in Maranhão as they did in Bahia, although the Revolt of Balaios from 1838 to 1841 against the Maranhão planters quickly brought together a large number of Negroes who thus showed their dissatisfaction with slavery and their desire for less severe treatment, if not for freedom. Slavery forms a common background for the Negroes of the two communities of Maranhão.

---

[39] "Forão presos o preto Militão, escravo de João Gomos Villaça por estar fugido, e a preta Gertrudes, escrava de Paulo Joaquim da Costa, por andar fora de hóra sem o bilhete de seu senhor."
[40] "Foi presa a preta Maria, escrava de Hipolito Xavier Coutinho por estar fugida."

CHAPTER THREE

Making a Living

Rural livelihood. Material life in the country today is very simple. The houses are rectangular, mud plastered structures thatched with palm leaves. In general, they have two rooms, separated from each other by a low, mud plastered wall or a wall woven of palm leaves. Most families keep a fire at one side of the principal room, where they cook and eat their food. Houses are barely furnished: a table, some crude stools, a chest in which to keep clothes, and hammocks or mats to sleep on. Utensils are few in number. Some households are provided with a couple of dishes, cups, forks and knives, manufactured articles of inferior quality. In most cases, the Negroes make their own forks of bamboo, and use rounded calabash gourds. A wooden mortar is used to shell rice, and iron kettles are used for cooking. Water is carried in manufactured pots or calabashes, on the head in the African manner. Baskets in which to transport rice, corn, cotton or vegetables are crudely woven of palm leaf fibers.

Cloth is scarce, and that which is available is a cheap material, generally bought at the village store. The men wear pants and shirts and have no more than two sets of each. Young women's dresses are only knee length, but those of mature women reach the feet. Women have, in general, only two or three dresses each, although a woman sometimes possesses an additional one of better material which she wears to go to Codó or to the social dances held in the village or in other neighboring rural communities. Few men wear hats. Nobody has shoes.

The diet is simple. Rice is the staple, and the Negroes eat large portions of it every day at the two main meals. Cassava meal, and a vegetable called *oushá,* which grows wild, are the two other daily items. Once or twice a week either pork, chicken, fish or the meat of an animal that has been trapped or killed by a hunter is available to them. Tomatoes, cucumbers, and pumpkins are grown by some families but are not often eaten. Though bananas and watermelons are well liked, the village people plant only watermelons. Their bananas, which come from the store-keeper's garden, they buy at the store.

Daily life in Santo Antônio is regulated by the course of agriculture, since its inhabitants, except for one old man and three persons incapacitated because of sickness, are occupied with their farms during most of the year. In addition, these people spend some time breaking *babasu* coconuts, which grow wild, to sell to the store-keeper. The fields are situated at some distance from the village so that the pigs, chickens, cows, and goats, which most families own do not harm them. A few of the Negroes own horses or donkeys to ride to their fields. A different plot is cultivated each year, the land once cultivated being then left to lie fallow, usually for ten years before being used again. A man chooses his piece of land to suit himself; no disputes arise because there is land for all. The total number of gardens is thirty-five, and these measure from one and a half to two acres, although some are as large as two and a half or three acres. Only four plots, cultivated by the strongest and most efficient workers, were of this size. The farmer usually plants his field in adjacent plots year after year, but he may, if he wishes, start a plot far from where he ordinarily raises crops. These consist of dry rice, cotton and corn, usually planted together, since the Negroes do not separate their crops by planting rice in one part of their plots, corn in another, and cotton in a third portion. When a man wants to farm a piece of land which adjoins one being worked by another, the matter is taken up with the latter and his consent obtained. A line of *mamona* trees is planted, or a wooden fence is made to separate the two farms. It is customary for a man and his adult sons to have their fields together, and close relatives or close friends often have their gardens close to each other.

Once a field has been chosen, it is cleared in the months of July and August. The trees are cut with axes, while smaller growth is cleared with a sickle. After awaiting some weeks for the trees and underbrush to dry, they are burned, the ash acting as fertilizer. Rice is planted during December and January. Small holes are made irregularly in the soil with an instrument called a *shasho,* an iron blade joined to a short wooden handle. Into these holes the seeds are placed. Between the middle or end of January and the end of March, the brush which grows in the planted fields is cut near the roots. Sometimes it is necessary to do this twice during this period. Though the hoe is known, the *shasho* is also used for this. Some informants stated that they had worked with the hoe but could not get used to it so they returned to using the *shasho.* In April and May, the rice is harvested, though at times this is not finished before the middle of June. In July, men and women break *babasu* coconuts, a task which is done in other months only at intervals when ready cash is needed. Corn is harvested in July; cotton of the previous year's planting, in September. Cotton planted the same year is harvested in October, November and December.

Rice is the crop most cultivated in Santo Antônio. Part of it is for house consumption, and the rest is sold. With the money from the sale of rice, cotton and *babasu* coconuts, the Negroes buy clothes, oil for their lamps, matches, soap, coffee, salt and sugar. Tobacco and a kind of rum called *cachaça* are two items on which the Negroes of both sexes, especially the men, spend a large proportion of the meager returns they gain from selling their cash crops. Though the Negroes say in Santo Antônio that "every poor man becomes rich in the summer" (that is after the harvest of rice), they have very little cash most of the year. An average family's annual income amounts to about seventy dollars. If the need for money arises, some people break *babasu* coconuts and sell them to the store-keeper, while others may hire out to him for pay given either in cash or in kind. It is not unusual for a man to have to sell a portion of the rice reserved for consumption by his family to buy clothes, medicine or other necessities. This indicates how great are the economic difficulties which many village dwellers have to face every year. Many persons complained about financial difficulties and their economic disadvantage and expressed doubt as to the returns which they would derive from selling rice and cotton. "Everything is expensive, and poor people have a hard time" was a statement frequently heard. Families often run out of rice for household consumption a few months before the new harvest, because the previous yield was small or too large a portion of it was sold. Rice is then bought if money is available. More often, a portion is borrowed from another farmer or, frequently, from the store-keeper. Before harvest, rice costs almost twice what it brings the farmer at harvest time, which means that a double portion of what was borrowed must be returned when the next harvest is brought in. Although the enonomic situation of the rural groups is thus precarious, it should be noted that their gardens usually assure them the items necessary for their subsistence. Furthermore, since their aspirations are limited by reason of their isolation from urban influences and by their own traditions, they do not experience their frustrations in an acute and permanent form and thus have no feelings of anxiety and insecurity.

Women and men alike work in the fields, the women helping their husbands or, more often, their *amásios,* i.e. the men with whom they live without being religiously or legally married. After their eleventh or twelfth birthday, boys and girls help their parents cultivate the land. The field of an *amasiado* couple is divided by a line of *mamona* trees into two parts, the smaller of which, about one third or a little less than that of the man, belongs to the woman. Work is done in both parts by the man and the woman together. The crops are divided in proportion to the amount of land owned by each. The rice consumed by the household derives mostly from the man's part of the field, while only a small portion from that of the woman is eaten, for she sells the larger part of what is harvested from her section. With the money, she buys various things for herself, clothes, soap, tobacco, and *cachaca*. She also helps with the household expenditures, buying salt, sugar, coffee, kerosene and other articles. The fact that she contributes to household expenditures does not in any way deprive her of her recognized right to the part of the crop which is harvested in her section of the field. Since the man may not touch what belongs to her, and she is free to use this as she wishes, she therefore enjoys a large measure of economic independence. This arrangement is common among couples who have not been living together for more than a few years. When such a union is maintained over a longer period, the garden is also divided in two parts, but there is no separation of the crops: an arrangement identical to that of married couples. In such cases, what is produced on the farm is regarded as a whole, part to be consumed, part to be sold. However, a woman always keeps the money she earns breaking coconuts, and disposes of it freely, and the contribution she makes to the upkeep of the family gives her an advantageous position which the man recognizes.

In cases of separation between *amásios* or between a married couple, it is easy to assign to the woman the part which belongs to her. The expectation that an *amasiado* union may not last is the reason unanimously given by those whose matings had continued for a relatively short period for the division of the fields in two parts. This is, however, not the reason given by couples who have been married or *amasiados* for a longer time, for such persons state that they continue dividing the land merely because they desire to see who has more luck, or in whose part of the field the rice grows better. It seems more reasonable to assume, however, that since they divided the fields when newly united, they continue to do this because they are accustomed to the practice, even though they no longer expect to separate.

As might be expected, women play a very active role in the economic life of Santo Antônio. They participate in almost every aspect of farming, abstaining only from such preliminary operations as clearing and burning trees and underbrush. They spend more time breaking coconuts than do the men. This activity until some years ago was considered an occupation for women only, and although men as the present time also break coconuts, at least one man expressed the opinion that this is not work for a man. The explanation for this change seems to lie in the need for ready cash, especially to have more money with which to buy articles necessary for subsistence. In addition to working in the fields, and coconut breaking, women also engage in fishing. In the months of September and October, when the river near the village is low, men and women together walk in the bed of the river and fish with nets. The fish are mostly consumed at home, only a small part being sold to people in the town of Codó. However, the return, which is small, only slightly increases the income of the Santo Antônio Negroes.

Cooperative work is common in Santo Antônio and in other rural communities in this region. The Negroes call it "exchange of days" (*trocar dia*). A man invites several people to work in his field, which means they are "gaining one day" from the one they are helping, since the latter "owes them a day," that is, he is obliged to work a day in the field of each one of the men who have come to help him. One of the men who has thus "gained a day" in turn organizes a cooperative group to work in his field. He summons the one for whom he worked, and perhaps some of those who were his companions, and so the process continues. Men usually "exchange days" with men, and women with women, but it is not unusual for a man to ask a woman to work for him on this basis. Some men, however, say they do not care to "exchange days" with any woman, because they feel women do not work as much as men. In general, however, it is believed that the women work as hard as the men: thus the store-keeper, who employs both males and females to work on his farm, pays workers of both sexes the same wage, his opinion being that women are as good workers as most men. Boys of thirteen, fourteen, and fifteen years "exchange days" among themselves when they work in their parents' fields or do odd jobs for the store-keeper.

There are no permanent cooperative work groups. Naturally, men have preferences in choosing work partners, kinship and friendship being the most important factors. Men and their adult sons, women and their adult daughters, brothers and sisters as well as more distant relatives in general "exchange days" among themselves, and friends are included in such invitations. A good worker, on the whole, likes to exchange labor with a man whom he considers as hard-working as himself. The size of these cooperative groups varies. Some consist of four persons: the couple who own the field and friends or relatives of each. Other groups may comprise six or seven persons, this being the number held most desirable.

Although almost everyone in the village participates in cooperative work in at least one form, individual variations are to be found regarding the frequency of participation in different kinds of agriculture activities. All Santo Antônio males join cooperative groups to clear fields, for this comprises the heaviest task that must be done, felling the trees, cutting the brush and burning the land. In general it is agreed that it is convenient to cooperate in preparing the fields, but some persons restrict their participation to this and do not otherwise support the cooperative system which, in their opinion is not advantageous to them. The reasons given for non-participation vary to some extent, at least in phraseology: one man held it was not convenient because the preparation of his own garden had to be interrupted while he went to "pay the days" he owed the men who came to work for him[1] to another, the men do not work as hard as he does;[2] while a third simply stated he did not like the system.[3] Those who prefer working by themselves, it must be noted, are hard workers who have the biggest fields cultivated by Santo Antônio people. It must be stressed, however, that most people in the village support the system, thinking it advantageous and taking pleasure in working as a group. They feel that the amount of work done is greater when they cooperate: "Trabalha aquela porção, o trabalho aumenta muito." The opportunity for pleasant social contact in cooperative work, indeed, ranks high in the list of incentives to participate in it. The workers, toiling near each other, tell stories, talk and laugh, and when they are in different parts of the field they shout encouragement to each other.

The Negroes who participate in cooperative work take their afternoon meal in the fields, eating food prepared by the owner of the field who may or may not furnish the entire meal, depending on a previous agreement. The most customary procedure is for the men who go to work in someone's field to bring their own portions of rice and for the owner of the field to have their food cooked for them. If the farmer furnishes their food, he, in turn does not furnish his own rice when he goes to work for those who worked for him. The meal is simple, generally comprising in addition to a large portion of rice, the vegetable called *cusha,* and pork, chicken or meat of some game animal that has been killed for the purposes by the owner of the field being worked. It may be noted that a man who is served meat is not obliged to provide it in kind when the service is reciprocated.

In addition to cooperating in agriculture work, the men also cooperate when a house has to be thatched. This is usually done on a Sunday morning or on the morning of a saint's feast day when no work is done in the fields.

---

[1] "Não convem porque o serviço fica parado."
[2] "Um parceiro não trabalha tanto como o outro."
[3] "Não me dou bem."

After the job has been finished, the owner of the house serves drinks to the men who helped him. Palm leaves, which are used for thatch may, however, be cut in the bush and brought to the house by men for whom the owner has worked in their fields, since this is also regarded as a form of labor exchange.

Urban livelihood. In São Luiz, lower class Negroes follow menial occupations for which pay is low. In consequence, they have a low standard of living. The men work as day laborers, or in factories, or as masons, shoemakers, tailors, painters, porters, stevedores, fishermen, gardeners, street vendors or employees of the city and state governments. The women are cooks and housemaids in the houses of middle and upper class whites; they prepare cakes and confectionery to be sold in the streets or in the market place by themselves or by their children; they do laundry for the white people; and a considerable number of them also work in the factories. A large proportion of vendors in the market places are women, and they make a picturesque sight in São Luiz, as they sit on their stools at the street corners selling cakes and fruits. Small boys and girls do light work around the house; when somewhat older, a boy is sent to a factory or to the shop of a family friend to learn some occupation. In such cases, their wages, for a time, are given to their parents.

Because they are subject to the vagaries of an urban economy, the Negroes in São Luiz are subject to variations in income and to continual threat of unemployment. Wages are small, allowing the satisfaction of only a limited number of needs, while their circumstances have been made more difficult by reason of the high prices of almost all articles during the past few years. The resultant insecurity is an obvious cause of the psychological uneasiness these people manifest.

Most São Luiz Negroes live in the outskirts of the city, in mud plastered houses covered by palm leaves. Notwithstanding the fact that materials used for house building are the same as in the interior, the houses in São Luiz differ in form from those found in Santo Antônio, and they are also smaller. Many of them have painted walls. They are furnished with tables, chairs and other cheap pieces of furniture. As is the custom in northern Brazil, hammocks are used in place of beds. Manufactured utensils are found in greater numbers than in the village, and urban Negroes wear better clothes than the rural inhabitants, especially as regards shoes, or sandals among the poorer folk. Their meals are much more diversified than in the interior.

Granting that women often make appreciable contributions to the household, their economic role is somewhat less important in the urban than in the rural setting. Women who are married or who live as common-law wives may not contribute at all to the family expenses, since care of the house and of such children as there are takes most of their time. An appreciable number do, however, make a contribution to household expenses and because of this, enjoy high economic status. As in the rural community, the economic role of the woman must be analyzed in its relationship to ties of marriage or of common-law relationship for, when a woman has separated from her husband or from her *amásio,* she, herself, must provide for her subsistence, as well as for that of her children.

The urban economy does not offer the same opportunities for cooperative work groups as does rural society. The pattern of cooperative work is not absent from the life of the Negroes in the city, however. In São Luiz, as in Santo Antônio, house thatching is often done cooperatively. The owner of a house to be thatched invites some friends to come on a Sunday morning and help him roof his dwelling. As the work is being performed, drinks are passed among the guests, and a meal is later served them. The work of thatching a house becomes enjoyable when four, five or six men get together to do it. In like manner, when the house of another man has to be roofed he will call to help him those whom he has previously helped or other friends, and they are not reluctant to come.

African ties. We may now turn our attention to the problem of identifying what is African and what is European or, better, Brazilian in the economic life of the Maranhão Negroes. It is evident that they participate in a typically western economic system. Even the rural group, which enjoys a relative self-sufficiency as regards food, is an integral part of the Brazilian economy, and it is through commercial transactions, both within the community and outside it, that the village people satisfy many of their needs, such as those for clothing, food, and medicines. The dependence of the urban Negroes upon money is obviously greater than that of the rural group, since the latter at least produce certain items which satisfy subsistence needs. The Negroes of the village work, in the main, for themselves; in the city, they are wage-earners.   ,

What, then, do we find to be of African derivation in the economic organization of the Negroes of Maranhão? That the high status of women and the patterns of cooperative work, important in both societies here studied, but especially in the village, are such items, becomes evident when we consider the historical connections between Maranhão Negro patterns and those of the specific African cultures from which they have come.[4] This conclusion is further supported by corresponding similarities already noted, which are found in other New World Negro societies: in Haiti, Jamaica, Trinidad, the Gullah Islands near the Atlantic Coast of the United States, Dutch Guiana, and the Virgin Islands.

In Santo Antônio, the slave women worked with the men in practically all agricultural activities. One elderly informant stated that the strong women were employed even for clearing the fields, an activity which is at the present time exclusively in the hands of the men. The women continued then to play a role in production under the slave regime comparable to that which their female ancestors before them had played in the tribal economy.[5] With liberation from slavery, the women continued working in the fields, a custom which was reinforced by the tradition that marriage ties were not irrevocable. The men, on their part, recognizing the magnitude of the women's contribution to production, conceded them their portion as a right.

The economic position of the woman in the urban situation of São Luiz is in some respects similar to that of women in the rural economy despite the fact that the dilution of African custom has been greater. Her contribution to the family income is in many cases considerable. During slavery, the women not only worked for their owners but, like the men, were also rented to others and thus became a source of income. In this manner, the tradition of woman's productive value was not lost in the city.[6] Furthermore, since the abolition of slavery, it has been reinforced by the inability of men, by themselves, to make livings for their mates and families; by the tradition that married or common-law unions may be broken; and by the sexual independence which women, by virtue of their high economic status, enjoy in this society, inasmuch as their income is assured them through the housework they perform for the white people, through labor in the factories, through selling in the market places and as street vendors, or through work as laundresses.

Comparison of our data with those for certain rural and urban Negro groups in other parts of the New World lends support to the interpretation here developed with regard to both Maranhão communities. In Haiti, for example, the women are not only the producers but the traders in the mar-

---

[4] These patterns, as previously shown in Chapter II, are found in Angolo, Congo and the Guinea Coast.

[5] This point is made by Herskovits (1941, p. 181) for Negro societies in the New World.

[6] *Ibid.*

kets, retaining what they earn to spend as they see fit.[7] In Paramaribo, Dutch Guiana, trading in the market place is also a woman's occupation and her gains are fully controlled by her,[8] while in Jamaica, Negro women also play an important role as vendors in the market.[9]

If we turn to forms of cooperative work, we may recall that these were found to be more important in the life of the rural than the urban Negroes. In the rural setting, as with the economic independence of women, African patterns found more opportunities for continuity than in the city. It is reasonable to assume that in the country the plantation system made possible the preservation of this tradition, since the men worked together in groups. Soon after liberation, say elderly informants in Santo Antônio who were themselves once slaves, the custom of helping each other sprang up. This may be interpreted to mean that the African tradition of cooperation found "a congenial counterpart in the plantation system," with the result that "when freedom came, its original form of voluntary cooperation was reestablished."[10]

This interpretation can be applied to cooperative work groups in several New World Negro societies. Thus, in Haiti the cooperative work group called *combite,* where men work to drum rhythms under the direction of a leader,[11] has continued the tradition of the Dahomean cooperative group, the *dokpwe.* In rural Trinidad, a similar group, the *gayap,* still exists, though it is not called so frequently as in the past.[12] Forms similar to the Haiti *combite* have been reported from the Virgin Islands and from Jamaica, while memories of large cooperative groups are preserved in the Sepoloe Islands of the Gullah group.[13] In addition, house building in Trinidad and in Haiti is a cooperative enterprise. In the rural community studied here, the system of individual ownership of property made of each person his own master and thus facilitated the preservation of the African traditions of cooperation and labor exchange.

[7] "The fact that the proceeds from trading belong to the woman who does the trading, and that in consequence women are encountered who, though married, command independent means and exercise full control over their resources, is a carry-over of African tradition and, as in Africa, this gives to women a position in the economic world quite foreign to conventional European practice" (Herskovits, 1937 *a,* p. 258).

[8] M. J. and F. S. Herskovits, 1937, pp. 12-13.

[9] Beckwith, 1929, pp. 43, 45, Fig. VIII.

[10] Herskovits, 1941, p. 161.

[11] Herskovits, 1937 *a,* pp. 70-75.

[12] Personal communication from Dr. M. J. Herskovits.

[13] Bascom, 1941.

supported
aproved

CHAPTER FOUR

The Family

In the two societies with which we are concerned, families are established either by legal or by common-law marriage. Marriage is, in general, sanctioned by the Church, although legal ceremonies sometimes accompany the religious rites. Even common-law unions, however, are sanctioned by both tradition and custom. That they are part of the cultural heritage of the rural and urban groups is indicated by their considerable number, and by the fact that they are accepted as normal procedure.

The fact that two recognized ways of establishing a family exist in these Maranhão societies make them similar in this respect to Negro societies elsewhere in the New World: in Haiti, Trinidad, Jamaica, Dutch Guiana, the United States, and other parts of Brazil. In Haiti, the institution called *plaçage* provides the means by which a man and a woman may establish a stable union, which, though without Church or legal sanction, requires the consent of the parents of both man and woman party to the match.[1] A similar arrangement is found in Trinidad, where the term "keepers" is given to the couple[2] and in Jamaica, where many Negroes live "as married folk without the ceremony."[3] In Paramaribo, capital of Dutch Guiana, a family may be established either by legal marriage or by mutual agreement between the two parties and their respective families.[4]

The Negroes of Bahia call this type of mating by the term generally employed for it in Brazil, *amigação* (*mancebia* in literary Portuguese). Such matings are widely accepted as a means of forming a family, although they are not as highly esteemed socially as the Church and legal wedding.[5] In Recife, common-law unions are common among the Negroes, many enjoying a stability which permits them to endure for long periods of time.

[1] Herskovits, 1937 *a*, pp. 105-107, 117.
[2] Herskovits, 1943 *b*, p. 399.
[3] Beckwith, 1929, pp. 63-64. In Jamaica, a woman who is being courted by a man "does not necessarily insist that the affair become legalized by a church marriage."
[4] M. J. and F. S. Herskovits, 1937, pp. 16-18.
[5] Herskovits, 1943 *b*, p. 399.

In a study made in that city, forty-two per cent of those party to such unions had lived together more than nine years.[6] In the United States, where common-law relationships are often set up among Negroes, "many of these unions are as stable as legally sanctioned unions."[7]

Rural families. In Santo Antônio, *amigaçãa* is the most common form of mating: there are twenty-four common-law unions as compared with twelve instances of Church and civil marriages and two of Church marriage alone.

Legal or Church marriage is marked by few ceremonies. A man about to marry has no obligations to his future parents-in-law,[8] and there are no formalities whatsoever associated with asking for the girl's hand. Church marriages are performed in the town of Codó by the priest or in the village during a visit of this officiant. The bride wears her trousseau, which consists of a white dress and a pair of shoes, which are a gift of her parents if they can afford them, or, if not, of the groom who, if he has had sexual relations with his bride during their courtship, is under obligation to provide her with a trosseau.

If a man deflowers a girl under twenty-one years of age, he must marry her, say the villagers; they state that such a man would be forced by the police to go to jail if he refused marriage. Intervention is secured by means of a complaint filed by the father, mother or guardian of the girl to the white man of the village who represents the police there, or directly to the police in the town of Codó. In fact, however, a man is seldom forced to marry a girl he has deflowered. If he does not wish such a union, he may leave the village for a period of several months or pay the girl an indemnity to compensate for the loss of her virginity.[9] In the latter case, the man is said to "pay for the honor" of the girl whose parents agree not to make a complaint; thus the contemplated action against him is not brought. The indemnity

---

[6] Ribeiro, 1945, pp. 44-51, especially p. 49.

[7] Johnson, 1934, p. 66. The same point is made by Powdermaker, 1939, p. 149.

[8] In Haiti, the bridegroom-to-be "must properly 'respect' the parents of the girl by helping them work their fields or performing other tasks, such as seeing that the men are called for a *combite* (though he would not be expected to provide the feast), or summoning those needed to do thatching" (Herskovits, 1937 *a*, p. 166). In Dutch Guiana, if the girl's parents engage in farming, their daughter's fiancé comes to help them when he is called. The attendance of the fiancé at the funeral and wake of a member of the girl's family is obligatory. He is also under obligation to help with the large expenditures for an important sacrifice to calm a spiritual being who is making trouble for the girl's family (M. J. and F. S. Herskovits, 1937, p. 17).

[9] Informants used the expression *"dotar"*—to give an indemnity.

demanded is from 100 to 200 *cruzeiros* in cash ($5.00-$10.00)—a considerable sum for the rural Negroes—or a cow, a horse or an ass. The fact that a deflowered woman loses her opportunity for marriage is at the basis of this custom, though the social value of virginity must be taken into consideration as well as its economic significance. This value is easily perceived in the feeling tone associated with the use of the term *moça* and *solteira*, the former being applied to an unmarried girl who is a virgin, the latter to an unmarried woman who is not one.

The parents' attitude toward a girl who loses her virginity is, in general, one of resignation, and in such a case, a common-law union would be accepted as a natural solution to the problem. There are, of course, times when the parental attitude is severe, as can be illustrated by the example of an old woman who said: "My daughter left my home to live with a man without my consent. I refused to give her my blessing for a year and a half." However, as is here apparent, even in such cases, reconciliation is eventually achieved.

The first alternative a man has for escaping marriage, flight from the village, is exemplified by a recent case. Josefina, after having had sexual relations for the first time with a young bachelor, Jorge, made a complaint against him to the representative of the police in the village. In order to avoid marriage, Jorge left the village with the hope that Josefina would have sexual relations with other men. If this were to happen, he would be relieved of his obligation to marry her or pay an indemnity. This expectation was confirmed, since Josefina became the mistress, *amaziou*, as it is said, of another by whom she had a child. The original offender then returned to the village as if nothing had happened.

Common-law union is established simply by a man and a woman living together and forming a new household. The following statements made by two different men illustrate this point: "I deflowered a girl, and then lived with her for eleven years. We just decided to set up housekeeping together." "Many women do not care about getting married. They live together (*amaziam*)." In one extra-legal union the two partners living together refer to each other as "companions" (*companheiro*), (f. *companheira*). Or a woman might call her mate "my man" (*meu homem*). The term *caseira*, applied to a woman who takes care of a house, is also used, but less frequently. The expression "to live in a state of marriage" (*viver maritalmente*) encountered in other parts of Brazil[10] is used by persons of education in São Luiz but was never heard in Santo Antônio. The term *amigo*, (f. *amiga*),

[10] Ribeiro, 1945, pp. 44-46.

amásio (f. *amásia*), as well as the verbs *amigar* and *amasiar* ("to be friends") are the terms most generally employed to characterize persons who participate in these extra-legal relationships.

In addition to this kind of mating, there is another extra-legal type in which the man and the woman do not live in the same house. It is said that the man "goes to the woman's house," that is, he pays her frequent visits, usually daily. In such unions, the interests of the parties concerned are primarily of a sexual nature. They lack the social and economic foundations of marriage or common-law unions and are usually of short duration. Yet some unions thus begun may become stable, in which case the man and the woman come to live together in one house in the manner of *amásiados*. At least five unions of this transitory type were observed in Santo Antônio and like the common-law unions, were socially accepted. In three cases, the women did not have any children, while in the other two. children had been born of previous matings. In these casess, where a man visits the home of a woman, the latter has as much, it not more, independence even than a woman who lives with a man without being married to him. The produce from the field of a woman who is "visited" is not shared with the *amásio*, though the latter has the obligation to help maintain her, and to clear the brush from her field. In one case, a man reserved a part of his field for the woman he was visiting; in another, a man paid a third person to clear a plot of land for her distant from his own field. On the other hand, in three of the five cases observed, outside help was hired to do this work, which seems to indicate that in this type of union, the help given by a man to the woman does not follow any regular pattern.

If an unmarried girl bears a child, her family does not expel her, even when the identity of the father is doubtful or when the latter will not assume responsibility. Two unmarried women, each having one child, were living with their respective mothers when this research was in progress. Also living with their parents were two women who had been abandoned by their husbands, as well as another who had been abandoned by her *amásio*.

Casual sexual relations and prostitution are not lacking in this society: it is said that a woman is "free" when she receives money or other gifts for her sexual favors. There were four such "free" women living in Santo Antônio, though they periodically spent some time in the town of Codó, where they were able to obtain more money for their services than in the village.

Although most couples are *amasiados*, many recognize the desirability of a union sanctioned by religion and law. There are several couples in the village who were married in a religious ceremony performed by the Catholic priest; civil marriage, on the other hand, occurs very rarely. Any explanation of the desirability of a religiously and legally sanctioned union must take into account the predominant moral and religious patterns, and the legal structure, of the Brazilian society, all of which exercise an influence on the village people. Despite the fact that the contact of these people with the white inhabitants of the city is only casual and superficial, the rural folk are aware that the custom held proper by the town's people is to marry and not live in an *amasiado* relationship, so that prestige accrues to this form of mating as it does to other customs and attitudes sanctioned by the Whites. Furthermore, as Catholics, the Negroes respond to the demands of the Church that people should marry.

Disputes over rights to the land in Santo Antônio have been a powerful factor in arguing the desirability of marriage sanctioned by the state. The three original signers of the contract by which Santo Antônio Negroes became the owners of their land left only "illegitimate" children, and these individuals are experiencing considerable difficulty in validating their rights and the rights of the descendants of the other purchasers who were represented by the three original signers. "Marriage by the laws of man" is thus set in opposition to "marriage by the priest" (i.e. religious marriage), the former being held more desirable because no difficulty ensues under it concerning the inheritance of land, or, indeed, inheritance in general.

What explanation can be given, then, for the fact that common-law unions are considerably more frequent than those having a religious and legal sanction? The reasons seem to be twofold. One must first take into account the economic situation of the rural Negro, whereby the expenses of a religious or legal marriage constitute a formidable obstacle to marriage for the members of a group who hardly have enough resources to satisfy their basic needs. In the second place, common-law unions form a pattern which is not only deeply rooted in the traditions of this people, but has a functional role in providing sexual gratification, economic assistance, and a family life which would otherwise be unobtainable.

Having discussed the ways in which a family is formed in Santo Antônio, we may at this point analyze the organization of the existing families, considering such matters as the degree of permanence of unions, the numbers of children, attitudes toward children, the disposal of offspring in case of separation, and kinship relations. The composition of the Santo Antônio families is shown in Table II.

T A B L E I I

Families of Santo Antônio

Married couples without children	1
Married couples with children	7
Amasiados without children	8
Amasiados with children	4
Living widow, or widower, with children . . .	3
Abandoned *amásias* with children	7
Couples of amasiados with children of the woman from a preceding *amigação*	4
Abandoned married women with children . . .	2
Married woman abandoned by her husband, with children by a present *amásio*	1
Total	37

This tabulation shows that in a number of cases, men and women have more than one partner during their lifetime, this number being actually greater than the table indicates since many of the men and women of the first four categories had participated in previous unions. This is indicated by the life histories of several of these men and women, by commentaries made by informants on sexual behavior in this community, and by the accepted patterns of sexual behavior as these are verbalized. It is regarded as normal for a man or woman to have more than one mate during his or her lifetime. Religiously sanctioned marriages, however, seem to be more stable than common-law unions, while the latter are of longer duration than the transitory unions in which a man merely visits a woman.

Most common-law unions are of short duration. In the preceding chapter is was indicated how the men divide their fields with the thought that the unions in which they participate may be dissolved. "It is a common thing in Maranhão for the men to abandon their *amásias*," was the way in which one person indicated the instability of these unions. It seems that the men play the active role in case of separation, but the initiative is often taken by the woman. Because she can care for her subsistence and that of her children, if there are any, she is under no serious economic handicap should she leave her *amásio* when she becomes dissatisfied with him. Furthermore, her chances of being a partner to another man are not diminished because she has been party to a previous union, for this circumstance rather strengthens her position.

In this connection, and in order to illustrate the normality of successive unions in this society, the story of a couple classified above as "*amasiados* with children*" may be given in terms of the experience of one woman who may be called Flora. Flora, who came from a neighboring village, had an affair with Pedro whose *amásia*, Alba, with whom he had been living for over ten years and by whom he already had two children, lived with him in Santo Antônio. Because of her *amásio's* affair with Flora, Alba abandoned Pedro and is today living in an *amasiado* relationship with another man. The relationship between Pedro and Flora was, however, transitory. They separated and Flora, who abandoned Pedro, became the *amásia* of Fernando with whom she has been living for the past eight years. She bore him four children, the oldest is now seven years old and the youngest two, and their union gives every appearance of continuing stability.

The cases in which a man and a woman do not participate in more than one union are, as a matter of fact, a minority in this society. Yet this does not mean that all matings are unstable or easily broken, for some endure until the death of one partner, this being true even in cases such as the one described above, which was not the first union for either the man or the woman. An example in point is that of a couple who have been *amasiados* for more than fifteen years, both having participated in previous unions. The woman had formerly lived with another man by whom she had a daughter. Two children have been born of the present union. That this was a very stable mating was indicated, among other signs, by the wish of the man to sanction it by a Church wedding, a custom followed by couples who have been living together for several years in other parts of Brazil as well as in other Negro societies in the New World.[11]

Although multiple unions are neither common nor completely accepted in this society, their validity is recognized. They are not condemned and do not form a social abnormality. Some men maintain two households: one for a wife or *amásia* and the other that of the woman he visits. Information was obtained concerning four such arrangements, only one being married. The woman whom this man "visits" lives in a neighboring village. The same is true of the concubine of another man who lives with his *amásia* in Santo Antônio. The *amásias* of the other two men live in the village. One

---

[11] In Haiti, "a man and women may live together as *placees* ten or fifteen years or more before they have amassed the necessary amount to pay for a legal marriage" (Herskovits, 1937 *a*, p. 106). In Paramaribo, children, and even grandchildren serve not too rarely as attendants at the wedding of their parents or grandparents (M. J. and F. S. Herskovits, 1937, p. 18).

of the latter has two children by his *amásia* and one by the woman he visits. The other visits the houses of two women and gossip has it that he goes regularly to a third. As his history illustrates the behavior patterns and attitudes which generally characterize multiple unions before their definite establishment, it will be given in some detail: Arthur, as the man will be called, "visited" the house of Antonia, who had a son by a previous union. She gave birth to another child as a result of her attachment to Arthur, who later fell in love with a young unmarried girl, Francisca, and went to "visit" her frequently. This greatly displeased Antonia. When Arthur reserved part of his own land for Francisca and told Antonia that he was going to clear a tract of land some distance away from his own for the latter, she broke with him. According to her way of thinking, Arthur was behaving incorrectly and should have given her the plot of land which he gave to Francisca. At the time of this research, the union had already been dissolved a few months, but relations between Arthur and Antonia seemed about to be renewed since he was paying "visits" to her. It was said in the village that he was also "visiting" the house of another woman who had been married and abandoned by her husband. She had formerly been Arthur's *amasia* before he turned his attention to the other two women.

Another case is that of José Silva who maintained such a dual relationship until the end of his life. He had lived with one woman, Altina, who gave birth to two children after she had already had one son by a former mate. When another woman, Ivone, came to live at the village, Silva maintained an *amasiado* relationship with her and spent most of his time at her house. However, he never abandoned the first woman. In the beginning the two *amásias* quarreled when they met, but as time went on, they accepted the situation and each led her own life without interference from the other. Later, they began to speak to each other and finally reached a cordial relationship.

Silva used to clear the field for the two women. Sometimes Ivone's was close to his, but in general he chose fields which were distant from his own, thereby avoiding undue contact and resulting manifestations of jealousy between the two women. At first he cleared the same portion of land for each woman, but as the number of children of his *amásia* increased he cleared a larger tract for her. When Silva died on the way to the latter's house, his body was taken there and not to the house of the woman where he had his "official" residence. A son of the first woman, Altina, said in regard to this: "When Dona Ivone arrived in the village and began to live with my father, he already had been living with my mother." Thus it was proper that the body should have been brought to her house, since this is the right of the first partner. But Dona Ivone and her child went at once to the house of Dona Altina, and together they kept watch over the body of their late *amásio*.

As seen in Table II, children tend to remain with their mothers when a union is broken. It is not strange, therefore, that children are generally closer to their mothers than to their fathers. The burden of rearing a child is assumed exclusively by a mother who has separated from her husband or *amásio*, and no aid is expected from the father or ordinarily offered by him. When a woman with a child from a previous union enters a new relationship, her new *amásio* takes the responsibilities, economic and otherwise with which the former *amásio* was charged. In some cases, a woman and her child, having been abandoned by her *amásio*, live in her parents' home.

The birth of a child is cause for rejoicing, and the father announces the event by shooting his shotgun in the air twice if the child is a girl and three times if it is a boy. Most of the children are, of course "illegitimate," a concept which the Negroes know but to which they attach no significance. "Illegitimate" children are regarded as normal as common-law unions, which is to say that no blame is thrust upon such children and they are not barred from full participation in the life of their community.[12] Indeed, the question of legitimacy is dismissed lightly by the villagers. As far as parents are concerned, children are treated affectionately, no matter whether they are born of a religiously married couple of of an *amasiado*. No matter what the type of mating, the father, as the disciplinarian of the family, does not hesitate to beat his children after they reach their fifth or sixth birthday if he thinks this is necessary to bring them up properly. That close ties continue to exist between children and their parents after the former reach adulthood is indicated by the fact, among others, that the children generally build their houses near that of their parents. Ties between children and grandparents are strong, and marked by a considerable display of affection.

An important relationship in this society is that between godchildren and godparents. Godfather and godmother are not only greatly respected, but are also regarded with real affection. In their turn, their attitude toward

[12] In the southern community described in *Shadow of the Plantations*, though many children are born of extra-legal relationship they are not considered illegitimate (Johnson, 1934, p. 60). A similar situation is found in Haiti, where children born as a result of an extra-legal relationship are not "at any social disadvantage" (Herskovits, 1937 *a*, p. 118).

their godchildren is kindly, though they can be severe when necessary. When a godfather or godmother dies, the godchild wears mourning for one year, as he would for the death of one of his own parents. Sexual relationships between *compadres* that is, persons one of whom is the godfather or godmother of the other's child, are taboo. Two people who have the same godfather may also not have sexual relations since they are considered "brother and sister by way of the godfather." In this regard, the relationship between them is comparable to that between true brother and sister.

Among themselves the village people are friendly, intimate and very informal. Certain forms of etiquette are followed by everyone. If a person meets an elder for the first time during the day, he immediately asks him for a blessing. Adults as well as children ask older persons for their blessing and often request this of each other even if there is not a great difference in their ages. Within the family, all children ask a parental blessing, while younger ones ask it of their older brothers and sisters. This form of etiquette, derived from the time of slavery, expresses the respect shown to older people and at the same time illustrates what is considered "good manners." Acquaintances and friends from different villages are greeted in the following manner: first a hand shake; then each one touches the other's shoulder with his right hand, and then another hand shake. Visitors from neighboring communities are well treated, and an atmosphere of cordiality surrounds social relationships among the villagers as well as between these and their neighbors from nearby villages.

Urban families. The terms *moça* and *solteira* are used in the same manner as in the village: *moça* is the term used to designate a virgin; unmarried girls who have lost their virginity and are therefore, more easily available for sexual purposes, are called *solteiras*. The proportion *of solteiras* in São Luiz, as in Santo Antônio, is considerably greater than that of *moças* and married women; the statement made by an urban informant that "the majority of women here are *solteiras*," proved to be an observation confirmed by the facts. In São Luiz the term *solteira* is even given to *amasiado* women.

In the city, most extra-legal unions are unstable, and the women who have participated in them do not have the same opportunities for a legally or religiously sanctioned marriage as do the *moças*, since virginity is considered a necessary attribute for a girl who is to be married. Due to this though a man may easily enter into a common-law relationship with a *solteira* he is reluctant to marry her, although this sometimes occurs. One man expressed the prevailing opinion when he said: "It depends on the friendship the boy has for the girl." This person, however, stated that he himself would not marry a girl unless she were a virgin. On the other hand, many men do marry women after having lived with them in permanent *amigação* relationship as was previously seen to be the case in the village.

Sometimes intervention by the Lão Luiz authorities, much more effective here than in the interior, obliges a man, under penalty of imprisonment, to marry a girl whom he has deflowered. More often, however, a common-law union is established in such cases. Patterns of sexual behavior, being as they are, the attitude of a girl's parents here also is one of resignation when an unmarried daughter leaves their home to become the *amásia* of a man.

In the city, as a matter of fact, marriage is held to be the proper manner of establishing a family to a much greater extent than in the case in the village, and it is much more common in the urban setting than in the rural community. The religious ceremony in the city is often preceded by the civil act, which is performed at the City Hall free of charge on Tuesdays. Weddings are also more elaborate in the city than in the interior, though this depends largely on the economic resources of the families of the principals. The bride's trousseau is furnished by her parents if they are financially able, or if not, by the groom; and a "decent" marriage must include a reception after the religious ceremony, when the married couple sit on a sofa and receive the congratulations of the guests.

Yet the matings which are sanctioned by church and state are actually no more stable than non-legal unions, for all matings are easily dissolved. Usually the two parties later form new alliances, the desire to establish a new relationship with another person often being the reason for dissolving the union. But this tendency, it must be repeated, does not prevent many matings, whether marriages or common-law unions, from lasting until the death of one or the other of the couple.

Urban Negro society is also familiar with multiple unions. A man will try to keep an "illegal" union secret, but in the majority of cases this is impossible. Finding out that her man has a secret union, a legitimately married woman or an *amásia* may threaten to leave him, and many times carries out her threat. In other cases, however, this does not happen and the man supports more than one household. "A man is able to keep two women and still live happily if he knows how to dominate them," it was stated.

"The first woman looks for the other (who is her rival) and has a fight with her, but if they are both respectable, this does not happen. In this manner a man does not spend money on prostitutes." The person who volunteered this information, a dark mixed-blood, thirty-seven years of age, who is a janitor in a Government office, had formerly live successively with three different women and, at the time of the investigation had two *amásias*. He gave forty *cruzeiros* ($2.00) a month for house rent to the second woman, who was a cook, and helped her otherwise whenever possible. The first *amásia* knew of his relationship, yet continued to maintain cordial relations with the second woman. However, the former abandoned this janitor after his second relationship had lasted for some months and went to live with a former *amásio*.

Another case, which further illustrates the pattern of multiple and successive unions in the city, is that of a shoemaker who was a drummer in one of the Afro-Catholic cult houses. He was married, and had a child seven years old. Before his marriage he had lived with a woman, to whom two children, both of whom died, were born. Later, however, he entered into an arrangement with another *amásia*, whose household he supported, for several years, and by whom he had two more children.

Granting that common-law unions are considered normal in this Negro urban society, and those who have lived together for ten years or more are regarded as being married, yet the relationship between *amásios* is not equivalent to that between husband and wife. This is well illustrated by certain rites of death for a married man as compared to those for an *amásio*. When a husband dies his wife wears mourning for a year, but an *amásia* does not put on mourning for the death of her "companion." The reasons for this vary. "It is the custom," said one woman who belonged to a cult house. "It is not becoming," was another reason offered. "It brings evil to the man's soul," was the opinion of a priestess in a cult house, who added that an *amásia* should not even have a mass said for the soul of her dead "companion" because this also would bring evil to his soul. However, such opinions are not universal. Some said that to give a mass for the dead "is a right that the *amásia* has," while others declared that the widowed *amásia* may even wear mourning. But the children of an *amásio* wear mourning when their father dies, for the fact that they are "illegitimate" is not held important in this connection. However, the city dwellers are much more aware of the concepts of legitimacy and illegitimacy than the rural Negroes, owning to their participation in the total life of the city and the taking on of the moral patterns of middle and upperclass Whites. "Recognition before the State," i.e., adoption of a child born of an extra-legal union, thus becomes one way to conform to the white man's code of morality.

Here, as in the interior, children always remain with the mother when their parents separate. For this reason, they are felt to be closer to their mother than to their father.[13] The significance of this procedure was stated by Herskovits in his study of Negro family in Bahia, where children also remain with the mother when there is separation.

So regularly does this method of disposing of children occur, and so recognized is it as the proper procedure, that it demonstrates the presence of a living, functioning pattern which governs this particular aspect of social behavior.[14]

Generally, the eldest child here is given to the maternal grandparent for rearing in the event mother and father separate, and in these cases the child is cared for with great affection. This is often also the case with a younger child. There is even a saying regarding a spoiled child: "He was brought up by his grandparents." Although it is preferred that a child be cared for by its grandparents, children are sometimes given to godparents, to friends or to white acquaintances, in case grandparents are financially unable to rear a grandchild or in the event that any of the persons just mentioned insists that the child be given him to bring up. Of these persons, the godfather is preferred, since he is considered as a "second father," and it is believed that he will be surest to take good care of his charge.

A woman who gives her child to another person to rear usually does so because of economic difficulties, and she may reclaim the child after a few months or even years, if her situation is relieved. In order to avoid this possibility, some persons only accept children if the mother, in writing, relinquishes her rights, the expression used by the Negroes being that the child is given *"de papel passado,"* that is, "by a signed paper." At times, the desire to free herself of a child born of a very short *amigaçao,* or of a casual sexual adventure, motivates a woman to give her child to another. In the main, however, children are desired, and many women meet with courage the difficulties they face in supporting their children. Thus several women stated that they would never give their children to anybody, some maintaining that adopted children are exploited by those who take them to raise, though evidence for this was lacking.

[13] "In Trinidad, Jamaica, the Virgin Islands or elsewhere in the Caribbean should parents separate, the children characteristically remain with their mother, visiting their father from time to time if they stay on good terms with him" (Herskovits, 1941, p. 180). The same arrangement takes place in Paramaribo (M. J. and F. S. Herskovits, 1937, p. 21). In the United States, the children in general remain with the mother or grandmother. Hence the name "maternal family" given to the type of the family that does not have a male head (Frazier, 1939, p. 127).

[14] Herskovits, 1943 *b*, p. 400.

Certainly the giving and receiving of children to bring up is a deeply rooted pattern in Maranhão urban negro culture.[15] And though it does not have a name, it is to be regarded as a true social institution with important functions in the urban setting, in contrast to the village, where it plays a minute role.

Relations between *compadres,* and between parent and godchild, are as significant here as they are in Santo Antônio. As in the case there *compadres* must not marry or have sexual relations, since any kind of sexual contact between them is believed to constitute a mortal sin. Sexual relations between a man and the daughter of his godfather are not approved and are also considered sinful. That this pattern is, however, losing its meaning is indicated by the statement of a girl who was being courted by her father's godchild that "this is the foolishness of old (*bobagem de gente velha*)." The relationship between godfather and godson is one of affection. The latter must visit his godfather and ask for his blessing three times a year: Christmas, New Year and Good Friday. A godfather is expected to help his godson whenever he can, in any possible way. If the baptismal godfather dies, the godson wears mourning for six months or a year, while mourning is worn for three or six months for the death of the *"crisma* godparent."[16] who is not as important as the former.

African ties. An interpretation of the Maranhão Negro family and of the behavior patterns and sanctions concerning its organization has to take in consideration the African background of the Maranhão Negroes and the situation of servitude to which they were subjected. As we take this approach, we must first consider the fact that the African slaves had to adapt their polygynous family arrangements to the monogamous system of their European masters. That this adjustment, difficult in itself, had to be made under very unfavorable conditions is one point that no student of life under slavery can fail to realize.

For one thing, the demand that the Negroes accept religiously and legally sanctioned monogamy as the only way to establish a family was but weakly

[15] The same custom is found among Jamaica and Paramaribo Negroes. In Jamaica, "sometimes one of the godparents will take the child for his own after it has reached an age when it is no further trouble to bring up, and in this case the child may never notice the parents again after it is grown" (Beckwith, 1929, p. 58). In Paramaribo, if a family is poverty stricken the child can be given to other persons to be brought up by them. This child is called a *kweki* (M. J. and F. S. Herskovits, 1937, pp. 21-22).

[16] *"Crisma* godparent" is the sponsor of a child when he is, after baptism, taken to the Church to be ritually blessed by a bishop.

enforced, as can be inferred from the small number of marriages among slaves. From this circumstance, of course, we infer that most slaves lived under common-law unions, many of them perhaps transitory. In this connection, it should also be noted that in the majority of cases the affiliation of slaves is recorded only on the maternal side in the *inventários* examined, which can be taken to mean that the father was a less important figure in the family constellation for the white owners, whose main purpose was to have a larger number of slaves. The role of the mother, magnified in this way, thus continued the African tradition according to which the woman enjoys a high status in family life. To these circumstances, which were not favorable either to the preservation of polygyny or to a change to monogamy, must be added an economic factor which was also an obstacle over the means of production, he inevitably lost the means of maintaining multiple households.

On considering the difficulties thus encountered by the slaves in the New World in maintaining any semblance of regular family life, one is tempted to agree with those students who feel that African forms of family organization could not have survived the slave system. Freyre says:

A escravidão *dezenraizau* (italics mine) o negro do seu meio social e de família, soltando-o entre gente extranha e muitas veses hostil. Dentro de tal ambiente, no contato de forças tão divergentes, seria absurdo esperar outro comportamento senão o imoral, de que tanto o acusam.[17]

Ramos is more to the point when he writes that due to slavery African social institutions were broken in Brazil, "os negros sofreram violentos constrangimentos o que *esfacelou* (italics mine) e modificou as suas instituições sociais." Following this line of thought, this student holds that common-law unions are mainly due to the economics of the slave regime, when he states that "a poligamia, ou melhor, a mancebia entre os negros reflete um fenomeno de ordem econômica, com bases no regime da escravidão."[18] Frazier, in his study of forty Negro families in Bahia, with the same orientation as Ramos and Freyre attributes the present family forms of the Negroes in that city, which are similar to those found in Maranhão, to "certain social and economic factors." It is his opinion that "there are no rigid, consistent patterns of behavior that can be traced to African culture."[19]

The expression "to break" (*esfacelar*) and "uproot" (*desenraizar*), used

[17] Freyre, 1936, p. 229.
[18] Ramos, 1943, p. 373.
[19] Frazier, 1942, p. 478.

respectively by Ramos and Freyre, as well as Frazier's interpretation, thus imply a complete break between African traditions and the customs of the contemporary Negroes in Brazil, including Maranhão. In Frazier's judgment, the Negro family in Bahia has been established as a "natural organization" created by present factors of a socio-economic order.

That socio-economic reasons exercise their influence in the establishment of common-law unions is clear to any student of the Negro family in the New World. In Bahia, for instance, in the words of Herskovits:

> the *amásia* mating is simple to arrange, solves the problem of the desire for permanent relationship and for children, does all this at an economic level which is within the reach of those concerned and affords a union that has a social sanction.[20]

The same can be said of common-law matings in Maranhão. However, we must not forget that the problem that is being considered is one of adjustment to new forms and not one of beginning a new institution. As we state our problem in this way, it becomes apparent that a tradition of forming successive unions rather than coexistent plural matings, a pattern started during slavery and continued unabated until the present time, provided the means by which the adaptation of a polygynous tradition to monogamic culture could have been, and in fact was, achieved. These unions, of the type now termed *amigação,* channelized one of the most deep-seated patterns of African culture and were at the same time acceptable to slave owners. Thus, to interpret such unions—most of them common-law—as a sign of family disorganization or demoralization can only mean that the student has lost sight of a most important mechanism in cultural dynamics: that of the reinterpretation of cultural forms.

Nevertheless, it must be pointed out that successive unions can, and often do, cause psychological tensions and insecurity, this being especially true in the city where black magic is a means often said to be used by women who wish to gain a man's affection. Both professional practitioners of black magic and, to a lesser degree, priestesses of the Afro-Catholic cult houses are said to be summoned for these purposes by jealous wives or *amásias*. In the interior, however, black magic is seldom employed to hold a man's affection. This, it is reasonable to assume, is because here the adaption to successive unions has been made more successfully than in the city, this in turn being due to no small extent to the fact that the rural Negro has been saved in his relative isolation from the cultural conflicts of the urban environment, where the Europeon patterns so continuously dominate the scene. In the

[20] Herskovits, 1943 *b*, p. 397.

same manner, mutiple unions are more common in the country than in the city. They are most readily accepted by the villagers and are not cause of as much conflict as in the city. This and the fact that the rural Negroes are not as conscious as the urban Negroes of the desirability of religious and legal sanction for their unions indicate that the isolation of the rural Negroes has made them less sensitive to white patterns of morality, and that the survival of relevant African institutions has been facilitated.

CHAPTER FIVE

RELIGION

Most of the Maranhão Negroes are professing Catholics. Only a small number in São Luiz belong to the Protestant and Spiritualist churches which in recent years have made efforts to proselitize them and have gained a certain number of new members. Yet, though professing Catholics, certain Negro groups in São Luiz, and most of the Negroes of our rural community, hold beliefs of African origin and participate in cult rites of African derivation. For, as in many other Negro societies of the New World, the acceptance of Christianity by the African slaves, and its transmission to their descendants, has by no means meant the disappearance of African beliefs or patterns of worship.[1] Rather they have been syncretized with the new religion; and it is with this process that we shall be concerned in this chapter.

The village Negroes have no church, and only occasionally go to Codó for a religious ceremony. One of these times is the festival held in January for Saint Sebastian, who keeps pestilence away. The devotees bring chickens, goats or money as offerings to this saint, and remain for the ceremonies in his honor. This and the visits made to the village by the town priest once or twice each year to officiate at baptisms and weddings constitute the constitute the contacts of the village Negroes with "official" Catholic religion.

Some persons among them, however, keep sanctuaries with the images of the Catholic saints in their houses. For *ladainhas,* that is rites wherein Church prayers are recited and hymns of the Church are sung, they join together at a house where there is such a sanctuary. The purpose of these *ladainhas* is to thank the saints for their protection during parturition, sickness and in other difficulties, or to honor a saint. During the month of May, which is "the Month of Our Virgin Mary(*Més de Maria*)," *ladainhas* are said every night, being at this time followed by a social gathering, perhaps

---

[1] Cf., for Cuba: Ortiz, 1917 and Romulo Lachatanere, 1942; for Haiti: Herskovits, 1937 a, Price-Mars, 1928, and Dorsainvil, 1931; for Jamaica: Beckwith, 1929; for Trinidad: Herskovits, 1941, pp. 221-224; for Paramaribo: Herskovits, M. J. and F. S. 1937, pp. 1-113; for Brazil: Rodrigues, 1932, Ramos, 1940 and 1943, Fernandes, 1937 and 1938, and Herskovits, 1942 and 1943.

a dance. Processions, to petition the saints for rain, are another form of worship.

African beliefs preserved by the Negroes in the rural community have been greatly diluted, so that only slight retentions of the elaborate religious and ritual complexes of Africa are found. These, in the main, are comprised of ritualistic dances during which the participants are "possessed" by certain spirits, and during which there is a "displacement" of the person's spirit by a supernatural being. The village people attend these dances, which are held at intervals of one or two months, either as participants or spectators, and beliefs concerning this aspect of life are shared by all.

At São Luiz, Catholic Negroes naturally participate in the religious life of the city: processions, prayers, masses and other religious ceremonies. Each year they join in celebrating the great festival for the Holy Ghost, the *Festa do Divino Espirito Santo*. In addition, many Negro families have sanctuaries at their houses where they may join together for *ladainhas* which are often followed by dancing.

African beliefs and practices have been preserved in institutionalized form to a much greater extent in São Luiz than in the rural community. These retentions are, in the main, carried on by groups of Dahomean and Yoruban descent, who have established cult houses that are the centers of African worship. The forebearers of the present members of these groups, approximately seventy or seventy-five years ago, established the two cult houses which today still continue to function under the names of the "Nina" or "Gege" (i.e., Dahomean) house, and the "Nago" (i.e., Yoruban) house. In Maranhão, cult houses are called *terreiros* or *casas* (houses) *de mina,* and the dances which are held there are termed *tambor de mina*. In all, the basic African pattern of possession and dancing accompanied by drums is continued.

In addition to these two houses, a Cabinda cult house also existed in the early days. It comprised only a few persons, whose relatively simple cult rites included possession. The person who told of this house still remembered the words of two songs by this group. According to her the words are Cabinda:

1. Tudi Batudi
   Etudi de.
   Etudi e Zembi
   Tudi de.

2. Tufamama,
   Oia[2] Zembi, oia Paka
   Elere.
   Oia Paka, oia Zembi
   Oia Paka, oia Mama.
   Tufamama,
   Oia Zembi, oia Paka.

[2] *Oia* is a corruption of the Portuguese *olha*. It means "look."

Of the words of these songs at least one, Zembi, can be identified as a deity in the Congo-Angola region[3] while the informant indicated that Tufamama was the name given by the small Cabinda group to Jesus Christ.

The original Dahomean and Yoruban cult houses stimulated the establishment of other centers of African worship, so that today there are twenty cult houses in São Luiz and its environs. The original Dahomean and Yoruban houses are located not far from each other in the immediate suburban area; but the eighteen more recent cult centers are distributed throughout the outlying suburbs and the rural areas, nine in the outlying urban regions and nine in the rural hinterland of the city. Yet in spite of the distance, some of these newer cult centers in the rural districts draw members from among city women. Of the houses located in the outlying suburbs, three were established between 1910 and 1920. During this period there were at least three other houses established which have since ceased to function. The remaining six functioning houses in the outlying suburbs were founded much later: from 1938 to 1943, by women who had belonged to some of the three extinct houses, or by members of the three houses established in the decade 1910-1920. Thus all of the nine functioning cult houses in the outlying suburbs have been directly or indirectly founded from the earlier period, and may be termed Yoruban-derived cult houses. Of the nine houses located in the rural area, four were also established by members of the Yoruban derived cult centers originally in the outlying districts of the city; but they were forced by the police to move to the hinterland because of their original proximity to Army barracks. In the five remaining rural centers, dances for healing purposes constitute the main rites. These centers have been established by practitioners of curative magic so that their healing ceremonies, which are forbidden by law, may be carried on. In such cases, cult dances serve primarily to disguise healing rites.

While all the cult houses have merged African and European belief, the Dahomean and the Yoruban houses are, from an African point of view, the most orthodox, though integration of African and Catholic beliefs and practices have been achieved in these houses as in the others, where, however, Indian elements have also been added to the rituals, a matter that merits further consideration in terms of the tradition of the use of magic called *pagelança* or *cura*.

[3] In the Congo-Angola region, the name is Zambi or Nzambi. Cf., Weeks, 1914, p. 276; Ramos, 1940, quoting among others H. A. Dias de Carvalho, *Ethnographia e Historia Tradicional dos povos da Lunda*, 1890, p. 517.

This *pagelança* is a dance, during which the *pagé* or *curado* (healer), who corresponds to the Indian shaman, is possessed by an Indian spirit. In this rite, he takes from the body of his client a thorn, a needle, fish scales, a lizard, or some other object introduced into it through the use of black magic. Participation in the *pagelança* by those who belong to the cult groups was not tolerated until a few years ago. Recently, a change has taken place and many cult initiates now attend these dances, and even seek out the *pagés* to ask for their help. Indian spirits are worshipped in most of the city's cult houses under the name of *caboclos.*[4] On the other hand, as mentioned above, there are five cult centers in the rural area of the city where both cult dances and healing ceremonies are held.

Catholic beliefs of Maranhão Negroes, like those of Negroes in other parts of Brazil, have much in common with African religious attitudes and patterns of worship, and this fact gave the Negroes a unique opportunity for amalgamation of differing beliefs and facilitated their acceptance of Catholic religion. This took the form of the interpretation of Catholicism in accordance with ancestral patterns, and thereby encouraged the fusion of parallel pagan and Catholic beliefs and patterns of worship. Thus, it may be pointed out that African beliefs concerning nature deities, personal spirits, the cult of the dead and magic have their counterparts in Catholicism. Nature deities are equated with the saints who control natural phenomena and sickness, concepts of the soul and the guardian angel with personal spirits, and beliefs regarding the souls of the dead with the cult of the dead. European magical beliefs and practices are also very similar to those of Africa.[5] In Brazil, the African slave encountered among the Whites a religious attitude very similar to his own. The saints were felt to be close to human beings, and to be easily reached not only in situations of crisis but also under ordinary circumstances.[6] Thus, their help was, and among some uneducated segments of Brazilian population still is, summoned to keep watch over confectionery in order to avoid ants, or find lost objects, or to promote marriages. The saints are, furthermore, treated like human beings, as is apparent when they are invited to be a *compadre,* or godparent, of a devotee. To the circumstance that the Negro found in Brazil this type of Cath-

[4] *Caboclo* is the name given in Brazil to a person of Indian-White descent. The same name is given to Indian spirits worshipped in certain cult houses in Bahia and Rio de Janeiro. In Bahia, such a cult house is known as *candomblé de caboclo, candomblé* being the name given to the cult (Ramos, 1940, p. 159).

[5] Herskovits, 1941, pp. 235-236.

[6] Freyre, 1936, pp. 21-22; *et passim.*

olicism Gilberto Freyre attributes the "deep blending of values and sentiments" which took place between slaves and their owners in this country. This mingling, in Freyre's words,

> difficilmente se teria realizado se outro typo de christianismo tivesse dominado a formação social do Brasil: um typo mais clerical, mais ascetico, mais orthodoxo; calvinista ou rigidamente catholico; diverso da religiao doce, domestica, de relações quasi de familia entre os santos e os homens, que, das capellas patriarchaes das casas-grandes, das igrejas sempre em festas,—baptizados, casamentos, "festas de bandeira" de santos, chrismas, novenas—presidiu o desenvolvimento social brasileiro.[7]

More than this, however, it is also to be pointed out that there is reason to hold that African beliefs very possibly reinforced the patterns of Catholicism.

Brazil, of course, is not the only Catholic country where this blending of belief took place. Lachatañere suggests that Cuban Catholicism has a special form among the Negroes, "estiéndase este Catolicismo de acuerdo con sus expressiones tomadas om Cuba,"[8] which indicates that Catholic beliefs were interpreted by the Negroes in accordance with their aboriginal religious patterns. In Haiti, the amalgamation between Catholic and African beliefs and practices is well known.[9] Parallel to the phenomenon just discussed is the process of reinterpretation, under which many Negro slaves in the United States adopted the Baptist religion, it being reasonable to assume that this religion, with its emphasis upon baptism by immersion, offered the Africans a pattern by means of which their beliefs and rituals connected with river and other water deities could be transmuted in terms of American Protestantism.[10]

Thus, it is to be seen how two religious streams, one Catholic and one African, plus a tradition of magic derived from the autochtonous Indians of the region, combined to make up the present-day system of beliefs and practices found among the Negroes of Maranhão. It is these syncretisms that must be uppermost in our minds, as we proceed to analyze the religion of country and city Negroes of the region as they exist today, for only in this way will we be able to understand the functioning system of belief and

[7] *Ibid.*, p. 263.
[8] Lachatañere, 1942, p. 15.
[9] Herskovits, 1937 *a*, especially Chap. XIV; Price-Mars, pp. 32, 38; Dorsainvil, 1931, pp. 35-37.
[10] Herskovits, 1941, pp. 232-234.

sanction that so deeply influences the lives of these groups as they are lived from day to day.

If in making our analysis, greater attention is paid to Africanism and Indian derivatives than Catholic practices, this is only because the former will be less familiar to the reader than the latter; and if, of the former, African custom is given in more detail, this is only because, aboriginally and in its present manifestations, it is so much richer than Indian religion. Let us, therefore, in moving from the better to the less well known, consider the formal Catholicism of these Negroes, then analyze the African and Indian derivatives, and finally assess the syncretisms, continuously comparing as in previous chapters, the manifestations of these phenomena in country and city.

Catholicism. The Negroes of Maranhão often refer to their saints without their titles, so that instead of saying Saint Barbara, Sain Sebastian, Our Lady of Good Parturition (*Nossa Sonhora do Bom Parto*), they will call them Barbara, Sebastian, or Good Parturition. This gives a clue to the manner in which both rural and urban Negroes, though holding the saints to be superior and supernatural beings, yet attribute to them human motives and desires and act on this belief to gain their favors.

Thus, if the rains do not come in December and January the rural Negroes organize processions around the village with the belief that the saints and God will send the needed rains. If, however, it still does not rain, a new procession is formed which goes to a neighboring village, and this time the images of the saints carried in the procession are left behind, in some sanctuary, while an image that was kept in this sanctuary is brought to Santo Antônio as the procession returns there.[11] This, it is believed, will bring rain, since the saints like human beings "feel bad because they cannot return to their houses," and will insist that God satisfy the petitions of the people, since only in this way will their wish to be returned to their respective sanctuaries be satisfied.

At times, when the urgency is great, the image may be placed in the middle of a planted field without shelter. "The saint is stolen," say the Negroes of this; in order to be released he will even more strongly beseech

[11] It was customary in nineteenth century Brazil for the priests to ask the devotees to organize private processions carrying the images of the saints of their home altars when they prayed to these beings and to God to end a drought. The images of the saints, which were moved from their altars, were returned only after the first rains had fallen (Moraes Filho, 1901, pp. 272-273).

God to send rains, because he cannot for long bear to be left under the open sky. Images of the saints are sometimes treated even less courteously, as when an image is trussed up with ribbon so that it will lose its freedom "to move." The devotee then tells his saint that it will be untied only after the rains come.[12] And since the rains in this region, though sometimes late, always fall in large amounts, the village people believe that the part played by the supernatural is a significant one. After the harvest, other processions are organized and the saints are returned with gay festivities to their sanctuaries.

This same pattern is followed to a great extent in the worship of the saints by the city Negroes. Though it is no longer customary to "steal saints" as it was some decades ago, there are still informants who tell stories about occurences of this sort. In one of these stories, "the little boy" whom Saint Anthony holds in his arms was stolen by a woman who desired the saint's help in order that she could get married. Today, women who sell fruit or cakes on the street corners sometimes "tie" the images of saints with ribbons, promising them to untie them if trade is good.

In addition, saints help their devotees solve their economic problems, ease childbirth, free them from danger and sickness, and in all ways play an important role helping man to find happiness. Each individual has his patron saint, who is usually "the saint of the person's name," that is the saint whose name is given a person either because he or she was born on the saint's feast day, or because the saint is believed to have watched over the mother at childbirth; or because the parents worship this saint.

The characteristic form of pledges made by human beings to the saints is not only that of a plea but at the same time of a contract. In essence, human beings exert pressure on the saints because they attribute to these supernatural beings selfish motives and thus offer them something in return for what they may do to satisfy a man's wishes. A promise to the saints thus implies that they will protect those who satisfy them, as can be seen from the following petition often addressed by city Negroes to Saint Joseph of Ribamar: "My Saint Joseph, if you will help me to obtain my wish, I'll give you a gift, and I'll light you a candle." Furthermore, a pledge given is redeemed only after the devotee has had his wish fulfilled, a distinctly African custom. On the other hand, these supernatural beings are believed to visit their displeasure on those who fail to keep their promises, especially if no explanation is given to them why a pledge has not been fulfilled.

In accordance with Catholic doctrine, the saints are held to be subordinate

[12] Saint Anthony and other saints are also sometimes "tied up" in the belief that they will help to find lost objects.

to Jesus and to God, and act as intermediaries or petitioners between them and their human "clients." "What God does not want, the saints do not ask," expresses well this aspect of the hierarchy in Catholic theology as the Maranhão Negroes see it.

The most important dates in Jesus' life, Christmas and Good Friday, are religiously observed. In the village, all work is stopped during Easter Week, and many spend their nights at the house where African-type dances are held. On the night of Holy Thursday, the story telling that began on Monday night is continued, the tales being of kings and princes, and many of animals having Rabbit as their hero. "Our Lord is dead," they say, "and we are attending his wake." On Good Friday, the women comb their hair only after twelve o'clock. Mourning Our Lord, they do not salute each other nor are blessings asked or given, before this time. These customs, which are not followed in their entirety in São Luiz derive from the time of slavery. Mello de Moraes Filho, who recorded Brazilian folk customs in the nineteenth century, describes this complex in the following passage:

O que se passava na Quinta e Sexta-Feira Santa no seio das familias era de uma simplicidade primitiva e tocante. "Porque Nosso Senhor estava doente," a casa não se varria, os escravos não trabalhavam, os meninos não faziam bulha. Não se cantave, não se dansava, não se tocava. As correcções corporæs eram abolidas; falava-se baixindo, jejuava-se, rezava-se . . ."[13]

Though the beliefs and rituals described here are essentially Catholic, the form in which they are expressed, as well as the attitudes that underlie them, can be understood only when similar attitudes and practices of West African Negroes are taken into account. Like the African gods, the saints are close to their devotes, are treated in an intimate manner, pleaded with and even treated brusquely so that they will satisfy human wishes. Among the Africans the gods, like the saints in Maranhão, serve as intermediaries between man and the Creator. Furthermore, Easter Week in the interior reveals the inclusion of at least one African pattern in the Catholic ritual, that of storytelling during the "wake" of our Lord, a custom which can be clearly traced back to Africa where stories are told to amuse the dead.[14]

In the city, the participation of Negroes in church ceremonies is very active. Daily church attendance, either at morning mass or at the evening prayer, is observed by a considerable number, especially women, while many

[13] Moraes Filho, 1901, p. 256.
[14] Herskovits, 1938, Vol. II, p. 325. Stories to amuse the dead are also told in Paramaribo (Herskovits, M. J. and F. S., 1936, p. 129) and in Jamaica (Beckwith, 1929, pp. 82, 84).

more go to Sunday or Holy Day masses. Four or five times a year the Negroes who belong to cult houses or to other groups pay the priests for reciting mass to honor a saint and ask for his help, and the relatives of a dead person always see to it that mass is said for his soul. Confession and communion, furthermore, are rites for which many devotees present themselves. Religious processions are principally made up of Negroes and persons of mixed blood, especially the processions of Saint Benedict and Our Lady of Victory, while the pilgrimage to the village of Saint Joseph of Ribamar, approximately thirty miles from São Luiz, to honor the saint of this name is an event in which many Negroes participate. At processions, both Whites and Negroes of both sexes are seen walking barefoot or carrying lighted candles, thus paying a promise they made to the saint of their devotion. The Negroes attend the same churches as the Whites, and both belong to the same church associations, which generally have the purpose of worshipping in the best possible manner the saint for whom they have been named. However, church societies with an exclusive colored membership exist in São Luiz as in other parts of Brazil, the *Irmandade* of Our Lady of the Rosary being the most important of these.[15]

Of the Catholic festivals of the city none is more impressive than the *Festa do Divino Espirito Santo* that is held in honor of the Holy Ghost. The Holy Ghost, symbolized by a wax pigeon, is believed by some to be God, the "Eternal Father." In accordance with this belief, Our Lady is held to have been made pregnant by a *Divina Graça*, a Holy Spirit. By some Negro groups, the *festa* is celebrated at cult houses of African derivation and one of the most impressive festivals for the Holy Ghost is held in the Dahomean cult center. Here this spirit is called Evo-Vodun, a term which is also applied to Jesus and God, and which in the Dahomean cult house signifies that deity who is above all others, *vodun* being the name for deity in Fo, the language of Dahomey in West Africa.[16] But whether in cult houses or elsewhere, the festivities are attended by many people.

Ceremonies for this spirit begin soon after the end of Lent. Every Sunday until the last day of the *festa*, a group of women meet together at the house where the rite is going to be held. Here, in the room that holds the images of the saints and the sacred wax pigeon, seated on chairs or stools, they pass several hours during the late afternoon and early evening hours singing songs to the accompaniment of double-headed snare drums honoring the Holy Spirit and invoking his protection. The women drum players, *caixeiras* as they are called, vary in number from four or five to ten or twelve.

[15] Ramos, 1935, pp. 86-89.
[16] Herskovits, 1938, Vol. II, pp. 170-171.

Before Ascension Thursday, a slender rounded tree trunk called "the mast" is brought on the shoulders of several men to the house where the *festa* is to be held, while the *caixeiras* sing and play their drums. Many persons follow the procession and songs such as the following are sung:

Bandeirinha branca,	Little white flag
Raminho da ventania;	On a wind-blown bough;
O Divino Espirito Santo	O Blessed Holy Ghost
Vai em nossa compania.	Come with us.

On Wednesday evening, the ceremony called "the erection of mast" takes place. This mast is put up in the yard of the house or, when the house is in a suburb, in front of it. A flag pole, the *mastareu*, to which a flag called "the flag of the *mastareu*," is attached, is hoisted to the top of the mast, while a wax pigeon is fastened on top of this *mastareu*. Before the mast, the flag pole, the flag and the wax pigeon are put in place, they are baptized by a man who acts as a priest; each of these units has its godfather and its godmother. The following song is then sung:

Vem de cá, Seu Padre-Mestre,	The priest is coming
Com seu livro do cração;	With his prayer-book;
O padrinho açende a vela	The godfather lights the candle
A madrinha poe a mão.	And the godmother rests her hand on his.

There is great joy during this rite, and much excitement. While the pole is being raised, the drums play though there is no dancing, and the *caixeiras* and other women present sing:

Ó Nossa Senhora da Guia,	Our Lady who guides us,
Vira a frente para o mar.	Turn your face towards the sea.
Me adjudai-me, meu Divino,	Help me, my Holy Ghost,
O seu mastro a levantar,	To raise your "mast,"
A levantar, a levantar.	To raise it, to raise it.
Eu quero subir ao ceu	I want to climb to heaven
Por uma manga de vidro	Up a glass stairway
Pra buscá o Espirito Santo	In order to find the Holy Ghost
Pra fazê festa comigo.	To make me this celebration.
Senhora Santa Ana,	Our Lady Saint Anne,
Prepare cuero	Make ready a diaper
Que hoje é nascido	Since today is born
Jesus verdadeiro.	The true Jesus.

Senhora Santa Ana	Lady Saint Anne,
Preparais mantel	Prepare an altar cloth
Para o vosso neto	For your grandson
Jesus do ceu.	Heavenly Jesus.
Senhora Santa Ana,	Lady Saint Anne,
Preparai as touquinha	Prepare a bonnet
Que hoje é nascido	Since today is born
Deus menino.	The God child.
Meu Jesus, meu Deus menino,	My Jesus, my God child
Quem lhe deu cordão de ouro	My grandmother Saint Anne
Foi a minha vo Santa Ana	Gave you a golden chain
Que tirou do seu tezouro.	Which she took from her treasure.
Santa Ana é maior santa	Saint Anne is the greatest saint
Que no mundo eu tenho visto;	Whom have ever seen;
Ela é mae de Maria,	She is the mother of Mary
Vó de Jesus Cristo.	Grandmother of Jesus Christ.

The following evening the *caixeiras,* in the room where they usually meet, again sing and play their drums, which are then given names, and baptized. Several flags of different colors, especially red, are also baptized. One of these flags, the largest, which has a pigeon inscribed on it, is called the flag of the Divine Spirit.

The last Sunday of the *festa* is its most important day. The group in charge of the festival on this occasion pays a priest to recite a mass in honor of the Holy Spirit, after which a procession is organized from the church to the house where the *festa* is to be held. The procession is headed by a boy and a girl who are called the "emperor" and the "empress." The boy, dressed as a page, carries the pigeon that symbolizes the Holy Spirit while the girl, who wears a long and elaborate dress carries a crown—the crown of the Holy Ghost. They are followed by boys and girls, and women, all carrying flags. The *caixeiras* play their drums and sing. When the procession arrives at its destination, all surround the mast and the *caixeiras* dance and sing songs of the kind already given, which glorify the Holy Ghost. The "emperor" and the "empress" then go inside the house and are seated in two high chairs which had previously been placed in the sanctuary, which now contains an improvised altar. The wax pigeon and the crown are placed on the altar and a *ladainha,* with musical accompaniment, is held, after which chocolate and cakes are served to all those attending the *festa.* Later, dinner is served and a social dance, a *batuque,* is held until early evening.

The *festa* ends on the next day when the mast is taken down. The *caixeiras* play and sing:

Graças a Deus para sempre	Let us thank God forever
Que o mastro se derrubou,	That the "mast" is down;
Meu coração estava triste,	My heart was sad,
Mas agora se alegrou.	But again rejoices.

Que pombo branco é aquele	What white pigeon is that
Em cima do mastareu?	Top the *mastareu?*
É Divino Espirito Santo	It is the Blessed Holy Ghost
Que hoje desceu do ceu.	Who today descended from heaven.

Then each *caixeira*, in turn, dances and kneels in front of the symbols of the Holy Ghost, the wax pigeon and the crown, which the "emperor" and the "empress" hold in their hands. A *ladainha* in the sanctuary follows. The boy and girl who play the roles of "emperor" and "empress" relinquish their posts to the two children, the *"mordomo"* and *"mordoma"* (royal butlers) who will be "emperor" and "empress" next year. Finally the *caixeiras* play and sing once again, to pay their last respects to the Holy Ghost, and this ends the *festa.*

Though these rites vary in detail among the groups who celebrate this festival, as, for example, in the number of drummers or the days on which the mast is raised or taken down, the *festa* is essentially the same everywhere in São Luiz. In it, religious and secular elements are combined in many ways. The *festa* has an important recreational function. It also gives social prestige to many who take part in it: to those in charge, to the drum players, to the godparents of the mast, the flag pole, and the flags, to the families of the "emperor" and the "empress" and to the families of the other children, the *"mordomo"* and *"mordoma"* who next year will be crowned. Those who organize the *festa* show pride, enthusiasm and joy in their achievement. Expenditures, though considerable, are met with donations made by many persons, Negroes and Whites alike, who are accorded the honorific titles of *festeiro* or *mordomo.*

The *Festa do Divino Espírito Santo* has not been held in the town of Codó for many years and, as far as can be ascertained, has never been celebrated in Santo Antônio. The reason for this, however, seems to be mainly economic, since it is difficult in small centers where resources are slight to obtain the funds needed to bring such an ambitious celebration to a successful conclusion.

Rural belief. African deities, in recognizable form, are all but entirely absent in the religion of the rural Negroes in Maranhão, but in their place are African-like spirits called *encantados,*[17] believed to "possess" certain

[17] The term *encantado* is used in the Angolan derived cult houses in Bahia and Rio de Janeiro where Indian, Angolan and Yoruban deities and the spirits of deified ancestors are worshipped. (Ramos, 1940, pp. 124-125, 159-162; Carneiro, 1936, p. 88, Chap. IV.)

persons during ritualistic dances. The *encantados* are said by some in Santo Antônio to be spirits sent by Saint Barbara, their chief, and by others to constitute a special kind of angel[18] created by Jesus. The *encantados* are held to be less powerful than the Catholic saints, but are believed to have the power to cure, to assure good harvests, to forecast the future, to aid in childbirth and in finding lost objects.

Another name by which the *encantados* are known is *budū*, which seems to be a variant of the Dahomean word for deity, *vodun*. Many of the spirits that possess their devotees in Santo Antônio at the present time have Brazilian names: Pedro Angaço, Carrinho Doeiras, Maria Bárbara, Manesinho, Baíano, Moça Fina, Trovão (Thunder), this latter probably being connected with the important Thunder deity of African theology. The highest *encantado* is the male spirit Kakamado (probably an African name) who is the chief of all others. Another is Kalunga, whose name has several meanings in Angola,[19] from where it comes. Some *encantados* that have African names, are named in songs sung at the beginning of the ritualistic dances, but they do not "descend" to possess anyone. These are Avrekete, whom the Santo Antônio Negroes call Verekete, and Sobo, whom they call Mother or Grandmother Soboa or Sobo, both from Dahomey. The name of the Yoruban deity, Eowa, is also in this category. Legba, the Dahomean trickster, here called Legua Bogi, is one of the most esteemed *encantados,* and some beliefs of Dahomean origin concerning him, which will be given shortly, have been preserved. In addition, the name of Lebara, the Yoruban trickster who corresponds to the Dahomean Legba, is found as a part of an *encantado,* a long name which, in its length, reminds the student of the African praise names:

Vai quando qué	He goes when he wishes
De vunso no pé	With *vunso* in his foot,
De João Barbara,[20]	He is John-*Barbara,*
Titinikati,	Titinikati,
Chaveiro-do-ceu,	Keeper of the keys-to-heaven,
Dûdû.	Dudu.

Though the Santo Antônio Negroes do not identify Bara or Barbara with

[18] In Haiti, spiritual beings similar to the *encantados,* the *loa,* are also called *Zanges,* a contraction of "les anges" (angels) (Simpson, 1945, p. 38).

[19] "Kalunga is a yet mysterious word which frequently recurs in the Bantu languages. In Ki-mbundu it has several meanings: (1) Death; (2ó Ku'alunga, Hades; (3) Mu'alunga, the ocean; (4) Sir; in this sense it is only used by the I-mbangala and some of their neighbors; in Loanda never; (5) sometimes an exclamation of wonder, amazement" (Chatelain, 1894, p. 294).

[20] The Yoruban trickster is known by the following names: Eshu, Elegbara and Elegba (Farrow, 1926, pp. 85-86).

the Yoruban trickster, it is significant that he is believed to keep the keys that open the gates to heaven, a trait suggestive of that Legba who in Haiti and Guiana is the guardian of the crossroads.[21] He is not identified with the Devil by the Santo Antônio Negroes as the Yoruban-Dahomean trickster has been identified in São Luiz and in Bahia;[22] but it is worthy of note that the Devil among Maranhão Negroes, both in the country and in the city, is usually called "the Dog," dogs in Dahomey being animals sacred to Legba.[23] This appellation may perhaps be due to the spread of the Dahomean pattern among Maranhão Negroes, an assumption that has the identification of Legba and Lebara with the Devil in São Luiz in its favor.

As among the Dahomeans and Yoruba,[24] Legua Bogi is believed to have his good and evil attributes. He is said to be good at curing or for finding lost objects ("é bom de serviço"). However, once he has helped a person solve a difficult problem, he demands offerings as a reward, with liquor being especially favored when he possesses his *irmandade*[25] or *cavalo* (horse) as the person who is possessed by an *encantado* is called, the latter being said to "mount" his horse."[26] One possessed by Legua, thus became the spirit himself, as in the case of possession by any *encantado* and exhibits a playful mood. The other devotees, in their turn, treat him with affection, and he is familiarly referred to in conversation as a resourceful and humorous trickster.

However, one who has promised him an offering or a gift and does not make his promise good, or any individual who may otherwise offend this deity incurs his wrath and is punished in accordance with the gravity of the fault. One way in which Legua punishes is by possessing the offender and making him climb a high tree, said to be especially sacred to him, the *tucunzeiro*, the culprit then being in danger of falling. He also punishes by causing a person to enter a thorny bush, or to run long distances without stopping, or to wallow in the mud. If the fault committed by the offender is such as to call for severe retribution, it is said that Legua may lead the

[21] Herskovits, 1937 *a*, p. 314. He is also so considered in Paramaribo (Herskovits, M. J. and F. S., 1937, pp. 67-68).

[22] Ramos, 1940, p. 137.

[23] Herskovits, 1938, Vol. II, p. 229.

[24] *Ibid.*, pp. 223-225; Farrow, 1926, pp. 85-91.

[25] Although in Portuguese this word means an association for religious or philanthropic purposes, in Santo Antônio it is applied to a person who is possessed by an *encantado*. This person is the *irmandade* of the spirit.

[26] The same expressions are used by the Negroes in Haiti (Herskovits, 1937 *a*, p. 146) and Paramaribo, where the women possessed by spirits during African-derived dances are called *asi*, a word literally translated by the Paramaribo Negroes as horse (Herskovits, M. J. and F. S., 1937, p. 74).

one possessed to kill himself. Thus, in true African fashion, Legua is capable of doing both good and evil, good to those who please him, and evil to those who dare dissatisfy or offend him.

Though no offerings are made to Legua as they are in Dahomey[27] or as in Bahian cult houses where sacrifices are given him before any ceremonies may begin,[28] a song is sung at every dance in Santo Antônio to send him away, though it is said, he does not mind the song and continues dancing:

Arretira o Lego,	Take Legua away,
Jalí, Jalo;	Jali, Jalo;
Adeus, Seu Legua ja vai,	Farewell, Mr. Legua who is about to leave,
Jalí, Jalo	Jali, Jalo;
Seu Legua e dono de terreiro,	Mr. Legua is the master of the *terreiro*.
Jalí, Jalo:	Jali, Jalo;
Arretira o Jara,	Take Jara away,
Jalí, Jalo;	Jali, Jalo;
Adeus, Seu Legua ja vai,	Farewell, Mr. Legua who is about to leave,
Jalí, Jalo;	Jali, Jalo;
Arretira o Legua do terreiro	Take Legua away from the *terreiro*,
Jalí, Jalo.	Jali, Jalo.

In reality, the devotees do not perceive clearly the implications of this song, for it is to be noted that Legua is here given the title of "master of the *terreiro*," which would seem to signify that he is one of the most powerful *encantados*.

The ceremonial dancing and singing to worship the *encantados* is known in Santo Antônio by several names: *pagé, brinquedo de* Saint Barbara, *tereko, nago* and *Budū*. The term *pagé*, the Indian name for shaman, requires some explanation. In São Luiz it is applied to persons who engage in magical healing practices of Indian origin. In Santo Antônio, however, no practitioners of curative magic are found, nor is the tradition of Indian magic more than slightly known. How the term *pagé* came to be taken over, and who introduced it, or whether Santo Antônio Negroes were in the past exposed to Indian traditions, are all questions concerning which information is unfortunately lacking. Though the term *brinquedo de* (play of) Saint Barbara is less used than *pagé*, it concerns the worship of the *encantados* more directly, since Saint Barbara is considered to be the deity who sponsors this worship. Here it should be noted that in Africa and some parts of the

[27] Herskovits, 1938, Vol. II, p. 229.
[28] Ramos, 1940, pp. 45-46.

New World, "to play" means to have a ceremony and "play" means dance."[29] The term *tereko* (of indeterminate origin), *nago* (an African word which refers to the language of the Yoruba of Nigeria), and *budū* (a variant of the Dahomean word for deity, *vodun*, as was seen) are heard still less frequently.

The dances during which possession takes place are held every month or every two months. They occur on Saturday nights, in a structure which differs from the other houses in the village in that it is partially open at one side, and they last until dawn. The pavilion where they are given has a principal room that measures twenty-five by thirty feet where the dancing is done, and another room inside, a sanctuary with the images of a number of Catholic saints and a wooden box in which are kept the sacred stones, that, according to belief, are the "seat" of the *encantados*, a belief widely distributed in West Africa.[30] In Africa, certain stones appertain to specific deities, but this is not the case in Santo Antônio, for here, where the names of the African deities have been forgotten, new identifications have not been made. It is believed, however, that the stones should not be touched, since an *encantado* will possess anyone who does touch them. No offerings are made to the *encantados* in this room, but once every year the sacred stones are ceremonially washed with water and wine by the men who direct the dance, this being an occasion for the devotees to petition the *encantados* for favors. The name *urna* (urn) given to the inner room just described, is a Brazilian term.

As in every other house, this one has a pole in the center of the main room that helps to support the structure. The dancers move about this pole in a counter-clockwise direction. Most of them who come to the dance are spectators. But at least fifteen adults of both sexes, the number of women being slightly larger than that of the men, customarily experience possession at a dance in a community with an adult population of eighty persons. Those who become possessed, together with others who are musicians or who are closely associated with the dances, are said to be members of what is called "the society" (*a sociedade*). In addition to these, there are some women who dance without being possessed, for the pleasure of dancing. Each person dances by himself or herself, the style of dancing being simple and uniform.

The musical accompaniment is provided by a single-headed hollow-log drum, its cow-, goat-, or deer-skin head being kept taut by pegs; one or two musical bows (*berimbaus*); and some rattles. The musicians are all men and they stand while playing. The drum, which is long, is placed between

[29] Information given by Dr. M. J. Herskovits.
[30] Herskovits, 1938, Vol. II, p. 244; Talbot, 1926, Vol. II, pp. 20, 22, 336.

the player's legs and is attached to his waist by a rope. It is played with the finger tips, the heel of the hands,[31] and sometimes the elbow. The *berimbau* is an instrument of Angolan origin[32] preserved by the Santo Antônio Negroes and found also in Bahia and other parts of the New World.[33]

The group which participates actively in the ritual for the *encantados* forms what perhaps may be thought of as a religious organization, though it is so formal that it can scarcely be termed that. It holds monthly or bi-monthly dances which are almost the only occasions for formal participation in worship. Certainly admission to this group requires no ceremonies of initiation, while drinking on the part of most "members" during a dance deprives the ritual of some of its sacred character, and acts as a disintegrating factor. The group even lacks the direction of an acknowledged priest, though there are two men who take charge of the arrangements for the dances, and have important functions during them.

. The functions of these leaders may be briefly indicated. They select the date for a dance, repair the drum or cover it when this becomes necessary, buy oil for the lamps which light the room where the dance is held, and direct the activities of the group as a whole. Members acknowledge them as leaders. They refer to themselves as "servants" or "chiefs" of the *encantados*, the latter concept being in accordance with the Dahomean tradition that the priest is the chief of the deities, as the word *vodunon*[34] indicates. However, these "servants" are not exactly priests, and save for their functions during the dance, which will be indicated below, they act in every other respect as any other member of the community.

We may now describe one of these dances and the ceremonies which antecede it. First of all, the main room is "blessed" by one of the servants." Water is poured on the ground near the central post and the four corners are sprinkled with water sprayed by a small branch of the sacred *esturaque* tree. This is believed to send away the evil spirits that might come to disturb the dance, among them the Devil—called the "Dog," as previously noted—is particularly envisaged. Then, at a sign of the "servants" all persons in the room prostrate themselves on the floor in the African manner, so that their heads almost touch the soil, and a "prayer" is sung by the members of the group asking for the protection of the *encantados*, inviting them to come to the dance and to possess their "horses." Either of the two following songs with mixed Portuguese-African words and names are sung at this time:

[31] The same as in Dahomey. See Herskovits, 1938, Vol. II, Plate 85.

[32] Carvalho, 1890, p. 365.

[33] Carneiro, 1936, pp. 112-114.

[34] Le Herissé, 1911, p. 129.

1.

La Varie, riero
O Keta eta e.
O Mina nuezõ, nuezõ,
La Varie, riedo,
Verekete usa no bão.
O Mina nuezõ, nuezõ
(the first five verses are repeated)
Mae Soboa nus valê.
(the same verses are repeated)
Pedro Angaço nus valê.

2.

São Varie, meu Deus
São Varie, budunso do lago,
São Varie, eiá.
São Varie, Jakamado,
São Varie, eiá.
São Varie, Senhovosapão,
São Varie, eiá.
São Varie, Mãe Sobo,
São Varie, eiá.
São Varie, Tinikaka,
São Varie, eiá.
São Varie, Maria Barbára,
São Varie, eiá.
São Varie, Estrela Ferreira do Ceu,
São Varie, eiá.
São Varie, Senhovunso do má

When the "prayer" is ended, the musicians begin to play and some of the women dance about the pole in the center of the room, singing as they dance. About fifteen minutes later, first possessions are experienced. In the initial moments of possession, the person dances at a very quick tempo, part of the time in front of the drums, part of the time around the central pole, whirling and sometimes falling on the floor or over the spectators. As the spirit "mounts" a devotee, the expression of his face is that of one in pain. He clasps his head with his hands, uttering loud guttural sounds while moving shoulders and neck forward and backward, his motor behavior being thus similar to that of the dancing of cult initiates in Dahomey.[35] The excitement of possession becomes subdued after this climax, and may end abruptly if the music ceases. In any case, the "servant" calms the excited "spirit," who by now has fully "displaced" his devotee's soul, by bathing the latter's head, wrists and feet with water into which leaves of *esturaque* and other trees have been steeped. It takes some time for the *encantado* to adjust himself to the body of the person he possesses, and it is believed that this bath of leaves eases the process, that it "firms" the *encantado* in the person's body. After this, the one possessed dances in a less rapid tempo. The bath is usually repeated in the "urn," the inside room, where the "servant" takes the possessed person after a time. There he is dressed in the garb of his *encantado* and later, the *encantado* is ritualistically sent away.

The *encantados* have their "uniforms," that is, their ceremonial dress. Some women wear a white blouse and a cap (*touca*). They carry a white

[35] Herskovits 1938, Vol. II, p. 116 speaks of "rhythmic manipulation of the muscles of arm and shoulder."

towel in the hands, or tie it about the waist. Some men also dance with a towel around the waist, but with torso unclothed. Others wear women's clothes if the *encantado* received is a female spirit, that is, long skirts, a blouse and a cap, and still other men wear a sleeveless blouse and cap.

After being dressed in their "uniforms," the possessed persons return to the dance space. Many of them make the rounds of the spectators, ceremonially greeting everyone present by twice making the sign of the cross, once on the body of the person he is addressing and once on his own, after which follows an embrace. The "servant" who has bathed the *encantado* is given a special greeting, the *encantado* kneeling and holding his head, kissing it as he asks for a blessing. This obeisance is held to be due the director of the ritual because, in the words of one of them, he is "the chief of the *encantados* on the earth."

A dance lasts the entire night. The songs, in the main, have Portuguese words, but African phrases occur, and African names of deities are mentioned, as seen in the songs quoted. Some songs refer to everyday matters, others praise Catholic saints, especially Saint Sebastian, others mention slavery while most of them comment on the activities of the *encantados* themselves.

1.

O Cativeiro, Cativeiro,	Captivity, Captivity,
Cativeiro me pegou.	I am in captivity.
O Cativeiro, Cativeiro	Captivity, Captivity,
Cativeiro o.	Oh captivity.

2.

Mamãe Maria Remadeira,	Mother Mary, the Rower,
Kokorio.	Kokorio.
Eu remo a sua canoa,	I paddle her canoe,
Kokorio ja.	Kokorio ja.
Dadae Mamãe Maria Remadeira,	Dadæ Mother Mary, the Rower,
Kokorio.	Kokorio.
Eu remo no ceu, remo no má,	I paddle in the sky, I paddle in the sea
Eu remo em todo lugá,	I paddle everywhere.
Kokorio ja.	Kokorio ja.
Dadæ Mamæ Maria Remadeira,	Dadæ Mother Mary, the Rower,
Kokorio.	Kokorio.
Eu remo no ceu, eu remo no má	I paddle in the sky, I paddle in the sea,
Eu remo aonde eu chegá	I paddle wherever I can.
Kokorio.	Kokorio.

3.

Ai Minajo	Ah Minajo
Rei Kakamado	King Kakamado,

Ai Minajo	Ah Minajo
Meu pai.	My father.
Ai Minajo	Ah Minajo
Meu avo.	My grand-father
Ai Minajo	Ah Minajo
Mae Kalunga	Mother Kalunga.

Requirements for admission into the dancing group, as previously indicated, are very slight. One has only to be possessed and to attend the dances, no initiation ceremonies being performed. Today, when a person is possessed for the first time, the *encantado* remains nameless for a period of one or two years. Then the spirit himself announces his name, after which he is baptized by the "servants" in the manner of common Catholic custom. Thus, naming the *encantados* seems to be a matter of personal choice. The persons who become possessed are required to abstain from sexual relationships on the day of a dance, while the meat of monkey, turtle or deer is tabooed to them. "It is bad for a person," they say, for he will be punished by his *encantado* if he violates these prescriptions. A possessed man or woman who is being punished by his *encantado* kneels in front of the drum and beats his hands on the floor violently until the "servant" orders him to stop. The same form of punishment is applied to a dancer when possession by his *encantado* is slow in coming. In order that the person may be possessed, the following songs are sun:

1.

O Biaia, o Biaia,	Biaia, Biaia,
Põe o menino no suador.	Make the boy sweat.

2.

Biaia, Biaia,	Biaia, Biaia,
Tu não larga o teu	You don't come
Pu be mdu aeio	You favor someone else.
Biaia uæi;	Biaia uæi;
Não larga o teu	You don't come
Pu bem du æio	You favor someone else,
Biaia uæi.	Biaia uæi.
Toca a chamada no mangericão,	Punish yourself
Biaia, Biaia.	Biaia, Biaia.

In addition to beliefs in the saints of the Church and the *encantados*, the world view of the rural Negroes also gives a place to magic. Foremost in their minds is the belief that it is necessary to avoid breaking certain rules if one does not wish to be victimized by a vague, indefinite, non-personalized supernatural power. Thus, the villager will say that "it is bad" (*faz mal*)[36]

[36] Prohibitions known generally as "*faz mal*" are common among the mixed blood populations of northeastern Brazil (Concalves Fernandes, 1938, pp. 75-83).

to do any of the following things: to walk over a place where an animal has rolled; to go between the wooden bars of a sliding gate; to pass under a fallen tree on the road; to sit down on the threshold of a house, over which many people pass; to thank anyone for a gift of tobacco; to attend, while ill, the wake of a dead person or to go to his funeral; or, if a man wishes to remain free of a woman's influence, to sleep with her on Wednesday nights or during her menstrual periods.

Asked why "it is bad" to disobey any of these rules, the villagers generally answer that "this is so," or say that they are following what their ancestors taught them, persons whose wisdom is not to be doubted. "It would break (weak) the body" to break any of these abstentions, for one would then be an easy victim to black magic or to diseases due to natural causes.

Black magic is known in Santo Antônio by various designations: *feitiço* (sorcery), *coisa feita* (thing made), *porearia* (filth) and *malefício* (evil deed), all Portuguese appellations; and by the term *muanga,* which is probably derived from Africa. Here it should be noted that the term *wanga* is given in Haiti to a charm of dark magic.[37] In spite of the number of terms applied to black magic it is only vaguely understood. No one who discusses the matter is certain how it is performed except that a practitioner takes from his potential victim an object of personal use, such as a piece of clothing and treats it in such way that it results in his sickness or even his death. It is also stated that insects, even an animal as large as a toad can be placed by a sorcerer inside a person's body, causing him to become very ill, this belief being probably due to the borrowing of an Indian tradition, which will be discussed later. However, only very few instances, and these outside the village, were cited in which sorcery had caused sickness and death. No practitioners of magic, good or bad, are to be found in the village of Santo Antônio, but the villagers know of *curadors* (healers) or "bush doctors" (thus called because they give remedies of roots and leaves) who are believed to cure physical maladies brought about by natural or supernatural means. These practitioners of curative magic also live far from Santo Antônio, in distant villages or towns. Yet, in spite of the effort needed to go to them, some villagers do make the trip. Their aid, consists in causing a person who has been sickened by black magic to expel through the mouth or nose the evil objects in his body that are harming him.

Charms can also be employed for good. Such are those almost always seen on small children. A little bag containing a tarantula or a crocodile's tooth is usually suspended from a cord around children's necks to avoid the pains of teething or to stimulate a child's appetite.

[37] Herskovits, 1937 *a*, p. 220 *et passim.*

The villagers also believe in the "evil eye" but they do not elaborate their ideas about it and fear it only slightly. And it is held that a man should not loan his muzzle-loader, used to hunt deer, rabbit and other game, because a curse may be placed on his weapon, and he will be unlucky in the hunt from that time on. Also in this category is the belief of Santo Antônio Negroes that there are men who can transform themselves into animals called *"lobi-shomo"* (werewolves) or, more commonly, *bichos virados*. These men are held to be sorcerers. When they take animal form at night they attack travellers on the road, or villagers coming home late from their farms. Several persons stated with complete conviction that they had been attacked by these beings. Their heads cannot be seen, their bodies expel an odor of sulphur, and they are extremely ferocious.

Of the beliefs here discussed, some at least can be traced to Africa, but their present form in Santo Antônio is very diluted. The concept *muanga* which seems to be derived from Africa is vague, and the use of charms is mostly limited to children. The belief in werewolves is both African[38] and European. The best explanation of provenience would be that the African slaves brought it with them, and that it was later reinforced by a similar European belief held by the Whites, while the abstentions knowns as *faz mal* similarly developed in the Brazilian setting under the stimulus of African and European traditions.

Cult centers. The cult houses in São Luiz where rites of African derivation are held are the private residences of the cult heads, their families and, often, of other cult members. In each of them, there are rooms for cult practices: a dancing space, a room used as a sanctuary with the images of several Catholic saints, and a private room which is entered only by the active members of the cult group.

The room with a sanctuary contains images of Catholic saints. Some ceremonials of the Church, especially *ladainhas,* are held here on the days when they are performed in connection with African-derived rites. In the Dahomean and the Yoruban houses which are located near São Luiz, a small rectangular veranda is the place where dances are held. In a Yoruban-derived cult house not far away from the near suburban area, a back room serves this purpose, while in all the other eight cult houses located in the outlying regions dances are held in a spacious semi-open thatched pavilion at the back or at one side of the residence of the cult head.

The verandas used for cult dances do not have anything to distinguish them from others, except a great many chromolithographs of Catholic saints hanging from the walls of the Yoruban center. Only at the end of the year

[38] Tauxier, 1927, p. 68; Peschuel-Loezche, 1907, pp. 343-344.

when the annual festivals are held is such a veranda decorated with streamers of colored paper hung from the ceiling. These are usually seen in the pavilions of other cult houses. In most of these pavilions, too, an altar with the images of several Catholic saints can be found near the back wall, between the two drums which are played at ceremonies. In all cult centers, the spectators of both sexes seat themselves on benches placed close to the walls, or stand near the low walls outside the dancing space. As the houses farther removed from the city are not provided with electricity, the pavilions are illuminated with kerosene lamps: only those in the suburban areas have electric light.

The private room is known in the Dahomean cult house by the term *pegi*.[39] It contains an altar, termed *pendomi* (like *pegi*, probably an African word), in the form of a low platform on which several stones are placed. The gods worshipped in the cult center are believed to be "seated" in these stones, each being identified with a particular deity. Several jars which contain the water held to be sacred to these deities are found close to the *pendomi*. In the Yoruban cult house, the stones are kept in a wooden box and a jar filled with water for Shango, the deity that is held to be the "master of the house;" the private room itself being known by the term *vardenko*, a word probably also of African origin, which is employed to designate the private room in most of the other houses, in only three of which, however, are stones found. In two of these three houses established more than twenty-five years ago, the identification of these stones with African deities is not specifically made, while in the remaining one—a center newly established—only one is found, that of the non-African deity worshipped by the cult head. In the remaining five Yoruban-derived houses, no sacred stones are found in the private room, but there is a rectangular slab; called the "stone of punishment" (pedra de castigo) on which the dancers, under possession, strike their hands when they have committed acts displeasing to their deities. This stone is no different from the one devoted to this purpose in most cult houses, including the two orthodox ones, since the form of punishment exacted by the deities is everywhere the same.

All São Luiz cult houses are organized along similar lines. Each is headed by a woman called *mae de terreiro* (literally, "mother of the terreiro," i.e., priestess) who directs a group of devotees of both sexes, most of whom are women. Of the latter, those who participate actively in cult life are possessed by the deities whom they worship when a dance is held at the cult house. These women are termed "dancers" or *mineiras*, a term derived from the

[39] The same form is used in the Bahian cult houses (Ramos, 1940, pp. 44, 64), and in the cult centers located in the southern city of Porto Alegre (Herskovits, 1943 *a*, p. 500).

word *mina,* which signifies those who participate in the *tambor de mina,*
(literally *"mina* drum"),[40] the name generally given to the dance.

In the Dahomean cult center, the cult head and the dancers are designated
respectively by the terms *hunbono* and *vodunsi,* the latter being the name
by which the cult initiates are designed in Dahomey.[41] There, its literal
meaning is "the wife of the god." Among the Dahomean group in São Luiz
it serves, as in Dahomey proper, to signify a cult initiate, but in São Luiz
on occasion its literal meaning is employed when a god speaks of the dancer
he possesses as "my woman" when he is actually possessing her.[42] *Minha
filha* (my daughter) is also used in the Dahomean and in other centers as
well. The *vodunsi* in the Dahomean cult house are further qualified as
vodunsi-hunjai, who are those who have been through a special initiation
ceremony, and *vodunsi-ahe,*[43] that is, those who have not. But these quali-
fications are rarely used; all devotees are generally called *vodunsi,* through a
vodunsi-ahe does have a lower standing than a *vodunsi-hunjai* within the
cult group where the principle of seniority is rigorously followed as in Africa
itself.

Not only are younger cult initiates subordinated to the older and especially
to the priestess, but the drummers are also organized in hierarchic lines.
Drummers are called by the Dahomean term *hunto* derived from the word
hun, the name of the largest of the three drums played at every dance in the
Dahomean house. The "chief-*hunto,*" who plays this drum, is the director
of the group of musicians composed, in addition to the drummers of the
gãto, of a woman who plays an iron gong, the *gã,* and two or three more
women who play rattles. This head drummer is directly responsible to the
cult head. His position, a very high one, is enhanced by the fact that he is in
charge of killing the animals offered as sacrifices to the deities.

In addition to seniority, a grasp of cult theology and a knowledge of cult
ritual counts very high in determining the position of a cult initiate, seniority and "preparation" generally going in hand. The choice of the present
mãe de terreiro of the Dahomean house, made more than twenty years ago,
was according to these two criteria. That they are still followed is indicated
by the statements made by several cult initiates and by the cult head herself
that the *vodunsi-hunjai* who will take her place—two rather than one—
have already been chosen on this basis.

[40] The term "drum" is used by the São Luiz Negroes in the sense of
"dance."

[41] Herskovits, 1938, Vol. II, p. 177.

[42] *Mina mulher* ("my woman") is, in Brazil, one way of speaking of one's
wife.

[43] In Dahomey, "those who have never been through the initiation of the
cult houses are called aye" (Herskovits, 1938, Vol. II, p. 177).

No Yoruban terms are used in the Yoruban or the Yoruban-derived cult centers to designate the cult head or the cult initiates. The Dahomean term *vodunsi* has been borrowed, though it is used in a slightly changed form, the Brazilian feminine ending *a* being employed, the word thus becoming *vodunsa*. Designations generally used in Bahia for the cult head and cult initiates, *mãe de santo* and *filha de santo*,[44] were heard only on a few occasions in the São Luiz cult centers. As in the Dahomean house, the older cult initiates enjoy a higher status in the organization than the new ones, who approach the former with great respect asking their blessings every time they see them. Immediately below the cult head in authority is the "guide"—a dancer who directs the singing during a dance, and who generally makes the arrangements for the dances. The choice of new cult heads in the Yoruban house is made, as in the Dahomean, according to knowledge of cult life possessed by a candidate. But in the two oldest Yoruban-derived houses, the cult heads who established these cults were succeeded by their own daughters. In the judgment of the priestesses and cult initiates of the two "orthodox" houses in São Luiz, the directors of the centers situated in the outlying districts of the city have but little "knowledge" and therefore competence, especially those who have established their cult houses in recent years, that is, between 1938 and 1943.

The drummers in the Yoruban and the Yoruban-derived cult centers are called *abataseiros*, which derives from the word *abata*,[45] of probable Yoruban origin. Each house has at least two or three drummers of its own, while there are always competent drummers not affiliated with any cult house, who are willing to play wherever there is a dance. The oldest drummer is called "*abataseiro*-chief" or "perpetual-*abataseiro*." In the Yoruban cult center, where sacrifices are offered to the deities, he, like his counterpart in the Dahomean house, is in charge of killing the animals. In all cult centers, the drummers cover and repair the drums and tune them up before they start playing, and enjoy a very high status in the cult groups.[46]

In most houses, the cult initiates number from fifteen to twenty-five, but the dances are not as a rule attended by all cult initiates. In most ceremonies, ten to fifteen persons were seen dancing. In addition to the cult initiates and the musicians, the membership of each cult house comprises persons who believe in the deities worshipped by the group, and are assiduous in their attendance at rituals. They consider themselves members of the cult house

[44] Ramos, 1940, pp. 58-60, 65.
[45] The term *bata* is used among others by Bahian Negroes to designate a drum (Ramos, 1935, p. 154; 1940, p. 239).
[46] For a discussion of the importance of drummers in Bahian cult life, see Herskovits, 1944, pp. 479-492.

and are accepted as such by the active members. They are adults of both sexes, but principally women. Men who play an important role as "sponsors and benefactors" of the cult, the *ogã* of the Bahian centers,[47] are not found in the cult houses of São Luiz.

Cult dancers. Every member of the Dahomean cult group, among which the deities worshipped are called by the correct generic Dahomean term *vodun*, "belongs" to a specific god, i.e. he worships his *vodun* and is under its protection. There are different ways in which one comes to "belong" to a given deity. Children who are born of women cult initiates, of musicians and of cult associates, are "given" to the *vodun* of their parent or to some other *vodun*, whom their parent fancies. Outsiders, who as adults become affiliated with the group acquire a *vodun* by choosing the one they like most; though if a *vodun* appears to such a person in a dream or otherwise indicates that he has been chosen by the god, the wishes of the god must, of course, be respected.

It must be made clear that the practice of the Dahomean group is to accept children of those who are cult initiates or musicians or members of the group for initiation into the worship of the *vodun*, who, it is believed, will not "possess" outsiders. As sometimes happens, should a person not related to some member of the group become possessed at a dance, she is immediately taken from the dancing space, since it is believed that the woman either was not possessed at all, or had been drinking, or the spirit that possessed her was not one of the Dahomean deities and thus ought not to appear there. To support this point, the members of the Dahomean group would indicate how different was the manner in which the person thus possessed danced in comparison to the dancing of a person to whom a Dahomean *vodun* had come—a difference that was actually observed at a dance visited in the course of this research, when an outsider did become possessed.

To be a *vodunsi*, a cult initiate, a woman qualified by relationship to a member has only to receive the *vodun* and dance for him, after which she is known as *vodunsi-ahe*, though, as mentioned, the term *ahe* is rarely employed. It is expected that a woman possessed for the first time will not perform as well as the others, and a more experienced *vodunsi* therefore shows her how to dance. As is done for the other *vodunsi* who become possessed, the new member is proffered a white cloth to tie around her waist or just below her breasts, and is provided with dancing sandals. She then goes inside the house with the other *vodunsi*, to return dressed as the *vodun* who possesses her, since she is no more herself, but this deity. After the dance is finished, the *"vodun"* all go inside the house and greet the newcomer, sing-

[47] Herskovits, M. J. and F. S., 1943, pp. 272-273; Ramos, 1940, pp. 69-71.

ing songs which express their joy that "he" (the god) has come. No ceremonies are performed, but the new *vodunsi* is supposed to remain at the cult center for some days while she is instructed, especially in the songs and dancing steps used by a *vodunsi*. By close contact with her group she will, however, in due time learn a great many essentials of cult life, and will thus become competent in her new role.

Should a *vodunsi-ahe* undergo formal initiation, she becomes a *vodunsi-hunjai* in which case she also worships, in addition to her *vodun*, a child spirit called *tobosa*. However, no *hunjai* have been initiated for thirty years, and only nine, the survivors of a group of nineteen, are still living. There are at the present time at least fifteen women in the *vodunsi-ahe* group. The chief reason given for their failure to become *hunjai* is lack of sufficient funds to meet the expenses of initiation. The rites to make a *hunjai* are, however, well-known, and it was possible to obtain from the priestess a description of the initiation ceremonies. The rites begin on a night of *zãdro and nahunū* two important ceremonies in the cult life of the Dahomean house, the *zãdro* being a ritual held in the *pegi* to bring on possessions by the *vodun,* while the *nahunū* is the ceremonial killing of the animals sacrificed to the deities.

When a group of *vodunsi-ahe* are to become *hunjai,* sacrifices must be ordered to all the *vodun.* At at late hour in the evening, before beginning the *zãdro,* the cult head, who herself is a *hunjai,* bathes the candidates' heads with *amasin,*[48] water in which leaves have been soaked, which is believed to free the novitiates from any impurities. When the gods are sent away ritually, however, the candidates remain lying on mats in the two inside rooms, where they stay for eight days, and are cared for by those who are already *hunjai,* who bring them food and bathe them. No one else may enter these rooms. Their only activity during this eight-day period of seclusion, except for dances in which they participate, consists in stringing white beads, called *kokre,* to make a necklace which can be worn only by *hunjai.* The skirts as well as the blouses which the candidates wear during this period are white. They may comb their hair but must not tie or arrange it. Ordinary dances, in which the candidates participate, are given on the two nights which follow *zãdro* and *nahunū.* On the third and final day of the three-day cycle of dances, there is a ceremony in the *pegi* where the cult head cuts a small portion of hair from the head of each of the candidates and offers it to her respective *vodun,* a symbol of the fact that the heads of those initiates belong to their gods. The *vodunsi* are now instructed by the *hunbono* (cult head) and the old *hunjai* about the position they are to enter.

---

[48] This is a Fo term that means "medicine." Its literal meaning is "leaves and water" (Herskovits, 1938, Vol. II, p. 263).

On the eighth day, the candidates and their preceptors come together again at the *pegi*. At this time the novitiates receive their *tobosa*, their child spirit, for the first time, as they sing the songs proper to the occasion. The older *hunjai* are also possessed by their respective *tobosa*, and it is the duty of the latter to teach the new ones how to "behave." The first time the *tobosa* come they are extremely shy and must be taught how to talk and behave. Like the *vojun*, the *tobosa* wear special customes. Women possessed by them put large colored cloths around their bodies, covering themselves from the breasts to the feet, and also are distinguished by shoulder-pieces of beadwork. During nine days, the new *hunjai* are possessed by the *tobosa*, possession beginning in the morning and ending at night. On their second day, the new *tobosa* announce their names, but no special ceremony is held at that time. At the conclusion of the nine-day period, the new *hunjai* have then the right to enter the *pegi* and offer to their *vodun* the sacrifices which previously were taken there on their behalf by their cult head, and by the other *hunjai*.

A year after initiation, there is a festival to "pay the head," as it is called. The newly initiated *hunjai* provide the ceremonies, and sacrifice to all the *vodun* worshipped in the cult house. In this way, they symbolically repay the elder *hunjai* for aiding and instructing them during the period of their initiation. Possession by the *vodun* during the dances, and by the *tobosa* after the *vodun* have been sent away, occurs during the days of this festival to "pay the head."

In neither the Yoruban nor the Yoruban-derived cult houses are the initiation ceremonies comparable to those in Africa,[49] or even in Bahia.[50] Furthermore, in some houses including Yoruban, members who have not been initiated, but who participate in the dances, can be found. This indicates that in some cases, at least, a woman need not be duly initiated in order to be allowed to dance.

This brings up the question: What does it mean to be initiated in the Yoruban or the Yoruban-derived cult center? Let us accompany a girl who becomes possessed for the first time as she attends a dance. In the Yoruban house, as in some others, a white cloth is brought by an assistant and tied around her body, though elsewhere a colored handkerchief may be put about her shoulders. She is then taken inside the house and dressed in the regalia of the spirit that possesses her. This spirit is generally known, as in the in-

[49] Although no description of initiation ceremonies among the Yoruba is found in the literature on these people, Herskovits' discussion of initiation in Dahomey (1938, Vol. II, pp. 179-188) applies to a great extent to the Yoruba.

[50] Ramos, 1940, pp. 66-69.

terior, by the generic term *encantado*. If the *encantado* identifies himself to the *mãe de terreiro,* necklaces in his special colors—if these are known—are added to her costume which is composed of a white blouse, large colored or white skirt and a colored belt about the waist. The colors of the beads generally follow individual whims, but in the Yoruban house one possessed by Shango must wear white and red ones, while white is demanded by *Yemanja.* If the *encantado* refuses to tell his name, necklaces are provided, but the colors have no significance. After the novitiate has been costumed, she returns to the dancing space and dances with the other possessed cult initiates until the dance is over, when her *encantado* is ritualistically sent away. That night, however, she remains in the cult house. If members of her family are with her, they will have been called inside to talk to the *mãe de terreiro* while the girl is being dressed as the deity. It is then decided, at least tentatively, whether or not she will be initiated. If the family is reluctant, the cult head and other cult initiates point out that the god has indicated by actual possession that he wants that girl to "belong" to him and to dance for him and that she will be subject to many dangers if the wishes of the *encantado* are not satisfied. She will be unhappy, and there will always be the risk that the *encantado* may possess her without warning, under inappropriate circumstances. Furthermore, other spirits may possess her and do her harm because her body is now weak as a result of this first possession. Weighing these circumstances, it is usually decided that the girl should be prepared to dance for the *encantado*. If, on the morning after her possession, the girl herself proves reluctant to continue she is convinced in like manner of the advisability of going through with the initiation.

She then continues in the cult house for the next eight days. She sleeps at night on a mat on the floor. If her possession occurred on the first night of a cycle, her *encantado* may return on the next two nights and cause her to dance again. During her eight days in the house, she does no work, but spends most of her time in a room where one of the initiates brings her food, bathes her and, in general, looks after her. After she has been in the cult center for some days her head is bathed by the *mãe de terreiro* with water in which leaves have been soaked. This liquid is called *veveu* in the Yoruban and the Yoruban-derived houses, though the Dahomean word *amasin* is also used. As this ceremony is being performed, the woman becomes possessed by her *encantado* who then announces his name, if he has not done so previously. Bathing the head, it is believed, causes the girl to become "firm" (*endireitada*), signifying that she will be protected by her *encantado* and will be possessed only during the dances of the house to which she intends to belong.

After eight days in the cult center, the girl returns to her home to resume her usual life. In common with the other cult initiates, however, she must follow certain precepts, very important among which is a taboo against eating certain sea foods. In the Yoruban house, as well as in the Dahomean, another important precept is that she will not sleep with men on Saturdays or during cult dances. In addition, the new cult dancer must save money to buy herself a ritual costume, at least a white and a blue, red or multi-colored skirt, a white blouse, a white cloth, handkerchiefs, a large cloth belt and a pair of sandals, though sandals are thought to be unnecessary in some houses. She also must obtain a rosary, which is bathed in *veveu* by the *mãe de terreiro*.

After the new cult member has these things, her *encantado* can be baptized. Two women, one possessed by a male, the other by a female *encantado* serve as godfather and godmother to the *encantado* "on the head" of the new cult initiate. The "godfather" holds a candle in his hand while still another "*encantado*" serves as priest. The Roman Catholic ritual for baptism is then recited after which the novitiate is a fullfledged member of the cult. In some of the Yoruban-derived centers, certain *caboclo* spirits are said to dislike baptism because they lose some of their strength, and cannot dance as wildly as before; but they are, nonetheless, also baptized.

Although the pattern manifest in the procedures just described is similar in general outline to the rites of initiations, as carried on in West Africa among Dahomeans and Yoruba, many important elements are missing and even those that have been preserved have been modified. The West African period of complete seclusion for several months[51] which is also found in the Bahian cult houses[52] is here limited to eight days, and formal instruction is reduced to a minimum. Actually, the long time required in Africa or Bahia to master the secrets of cult life is unnecessary, since cult life is here much less complex. Furthermore, the songs and dance rhythms are already reasonably familiar to all those who frequent cult dances, with the result that, during initiation, this phase of ritual instruction may be less elaborate. Cult initiates are not required to shave their hair as in Africa or Bahia.[53] In the Dahomean house, it has been indicated that a small portion of a woman's hair is cut off. However, members of this house stated that in time past it was customary to cut the hair of the candidates very short. However, the members of the Yoruban house used to shave their hair in old times, but this custom has been discontinued, since, according to the informants, "it

[51] Herskovits, 1938, Vol. II, pp. 180-181.
[52] Ramos, 1940, pp. 66-67.
[53] Herskovits, 1938, Vol. II, p. 185; Ramos, 1940, pp. 66-67.

would be terrible to do a thing like that nowadays as everybody would notice and criticize it." The important ceremony of "selling the slaves,"[54] that is, the cult initiates, in Dahomey, or of buying the novitiates as practiced in Bahia[55] is lacking in the Dahomean, Yoruban or Yoruban-derived houses, and no sacrifices are made on this occasion.

It seems reasonable to assume that the urban setting has prevented the continuation of some aspects of the initiatory rites, for even the procedure described is not followed in all instances, since many of the women must make their own livings and fear to lose their jobs if they absent themselves during the period of seclusion. In this case, the initiation may be interrupted to be continued later or not at all.

Cult gods. The gods worshipped in the Dahomean house are African and are identified as such. They have the same names as in Dahomey itself, and, as in the land of their origin, are organized into pantheons. Some modifications of West African practices are to be noted, but they are not very great in view of the degree of retention manifested in the worship of this group. Thus, whereas Dahomey has the three pantheons of the Sky, headed by Mawu-Lisa, the Earth, under Sagbata, and Thunder, of which Kevioso is the chief god, *vodun* in the Dahomean cult house in São Luiz are classified as belonging to three "families:" that of Davise or Dahome, that does not correspond to any of the pantheons in Dahomean belief; the "family" of Da or Danbira that has the same attributes as the Dahomean Sagbata pantheon; and the Kevioso group. These are generic terms for groups of deities as are their counterparts in Dahomey.[56]

In the mythology of the Dahomean house, the chief of all *vodun* is held to be Dadaho. He has a wife, Nae or Neadona,[57] and a son Koisinakaba or Dehuesina. Koisinakaba also has a son, Zomadonu, the chief of the Dahome or Davise family, who rules over all other *vodun* in the name of his grandfather, Dadaho, who has delegated him powers to rule. This pattern is the same as that followed by the pantheons in Dahomey.[58] Zomadonu has no wife, but has three brothers, Agongonu, Zaka and Dosu. The male deities named Bedegar, Dako, Tosa and Tose, and Dosupe, and the female gods, Akuevi and Sepazin are the other members of this "family." They are also said to form a group in their own right, the *tokhueni*, thought of as young deities.

[54] Herskovits, 1938, Vol. II, p. 188.
[55] Ramos, 1940, p. 68.
[56] Herskovits, 1938, Vol. II, pp. 101, 139, 150.
[57] *Nae is* perhaps the Dahomean goddess of the sea, Naete (*Ibid.,* pp. 151-152). The ending *dona* in the name Naedona is probably the Portuguese word *dona,* used in addressing a grown woman.
[58] *Ibid.,* Chap. XXVI *et passim.*

It is noteworthy that the names of the deities just mentioned are strikingly similar to, when not identical with, those of the kings of Dahomey. Dadaho itself is a compound of the words *dada*, "king,"[59] and *daho* "the eldest."[60] Koisinakaba seems also to be a composite name, the elements in it being first Koisi and then Akaba, the name of the King who ruled over Dahomey from 1680 to 1708.[61] Koisi is probably a "praised name" of this king since the giving of praise names is as deep seated in Dahomey as elsewhere in West Africa. Further evidence that Koisinakaba is Akaba lies in the fact that Zomadonu, in Maranhão held to be his son, was actually the son of the Dahomean King Akaba, worshipped in that African country as the abnormal royal child who heads the powerful group of all normal children born to Dahomean kings, the *tohosu*.[62] Agongonu as previously indicated,[63] is obviously Agongolo or Agongoro who ruled Dahomey in the late part of the eighteenth century and the early part of the nineteenth; Dako is the king of the same name who reigned from 1625 to about 1640;[64] and Dosu[65] may be identified as Agadja, since Dosu's second name, is pronounced Agaja in the Dahomean cult house of São Luiz. Agadja was the Dahomean king who ruled in the early part of the eighteenth century.[66]

The Maranhão Dahomean group is unaware that these deities have the names of Dahomean kings, but it is difficult to believe that this was not known to their forebears. In Dahomey, the deification and worship of the royal ancestors is one of the most important phases of Dahomean belief and ritual.[67] And while this particular aspect of Dahomean tradition is no longer found in Maranhão, the fact that the names of Dahomean kings are given to deities worshipped by the Dahomean group is sufficient proof that the worship of these Dahomean royal figures is being carried on today by this group in Brazil, albeit unwittingly. The especial significance of this survival becomes apparent when we consider that though a number of other groups of Dahomean descent have been studied in the New World, only the São Luiz group has continued this tradition.

It is further significant that Zomadonu, Agongonu, Zaka and Dosu Agaja

[59] Le Herissé, 1911, p. 5.
[60] *Ibid.*, p. 9.
[61] Herskovits, 1938, Vol. I, p. 13.
[62] *Ibid.*, pp. 230-232.
[63] See above, p. 14.
[64] Herskovits, 1938, Vol. I, p. 13.
[65] *Dosu* is the name given in Dahomey to the child born after twins (*Ibid.*, p. 272).
[66] *Ibid.*, p. 13.
[67] *Ibid.*, Vol. II, Chap. XXIV.

are in Maranhão given the generic term Savalunu, the name of the land where they are said to have originated—Savalu is in Africa, an important center and another name for the northern part of Dahomey, the Mahi country.[68] It was there, in accordance with the historical account given by Le Herissé that the worship of the *tohosu*, that is, the spirits of the abnormally-born children (that are headed by Zumadunu),[69] was begun.[70] The custom of giving the name of the place where the worship of a deity or group of deities has originated to the deities themselves is deeply rooted in Dahomean culture, and also obtains in the case of the Maranhão deity Ajauto de Aladanu, Ajahuto being in Dahomey the deified ancestor of the people of Allada, the Aladonu.[71] The name Aladanu is also given by the Maranhão Dahomean group to another of their deities, Podibogi, one of the main deities of the Danbira family. In the song for this deity the name Aladanu is often mentioned:

> Sale Bajobo Aladanu
> Ne Solusa le
> Jojo Honuma Aladanu
> Ne Solusa le Bajobo Aladanu
> Ne Solusa le.

The pantheon of Dã, Danbira or Odã is headed by Akosa Sapata, the same Sagbata who is chief of the Earth pantheon in Dahomey. By the Dahomeans, Dã is believed to be a serpent,[72] and this belief has been maintained in Maranhão as has been that which holds Sapata to be the deity who sends skin diseases as a punishment or frees devotees from these diseases as a reward. The Dahomean group in São Luiz believe Sapata has many children: Podibogi, Lepon, Aloge, Bagono, Aboju, Abototoe, Bosuko (all males) and Hueji, Bosalebe, Bosa, and Eowa (females). Eowa, however, is no longer worshipped by the Dahomean group, though in the Yoruban center she still has her cult, this being logical because her name really derives from the Yoruban culture.

As in Africa, Kevioso is the name of a pantheon as well as of a *vodun*. As a *vodun*, he is also called Bade. The members of this pantheon, all male deities except the last two, are Kevioso or Bade, Avrekete who is called Verekete, Loko, Lisa, Avrejo, Ajauto, Ajanutoe, Topodu, and Sobo and Abe.

[68] *Ibid.*, pp. 24-25, 144.
[69] *Ibid.*, Vol. I, p. 262.
[70] Le Herissé, 1911, pp. 121-123.
[71] *Ibid.*, pp. 103, 105, 111-112.
[72] Herskovits, 1938, Vol. II. Chap. XXX, especially p. 248.

The attributes of this pantheon are identical with those of the Hevioso pantheon among the Dahomeans, where it controls the thunder, rain and all bodies of water. Sobo and Bade direct the thunder, rain and all bodies of water. Sobo and Bade direct the thunder, while Abe controls waters of the sea, as in Dahomey where, however, she is held to be a male deity.[73] However, not all the deities mentioned by the Maranhão Dahoman cult group as belonging to the Kevioso family are so classified in Dahomey. This applies especially to Lisa, to whom reference was made previously, who in Dahomey is the high Sun god,[74] and to Avrejo, Ajanutoe and Ajauto. Furthermore, an important difference between Maranhão and Dahomean belief exists concerning Sobo, since it is held by the Marañhao Dahomean group that this deity is "an old virgin," a concept which is entirely foreign to Dahomean belief. In Maranhão, it is further said, unlike Dahomey, that Sobo reared Kevioso and that all other *vodun* in his pantheon are his brothers.

The Dahomeon cult group of São Luiz also follow Dahomean theology in their belief that the youngest deity of each pantheon is a trickster,[75] whom they hold to be an indulged or "spoiled" *vodun*. Each of these "spoiled" *vodun* is believed to be protected in his mischievous acts from the wrath of his father, the pantheon head, by a benevolent sister or brother. Bosuko, the "spoiled *vodun* of the Danbira "family," is thus under the protection of his sister Bosa; Verekete, the youngest of the Kevioso "family by his sister Abe;[76] and Tosa, the trickster deity of the Davise group, is shielded from his father by an older brother, Huandolo.

In the light of the fact that the Dahomean tradition concerning the trickster has thus been so strongly maintained, it is surprising to find that the complex of beliefs and practices surrounding Legba, the Dahomean trickster *par excellence*, has apparently been lost by the Dahomean cult group in São Luiz. Though repeated attempts were made when talking to members of this group to clarify this puzzling fact, nothing comparable to Dahomean material could be obtained, nor did the observation of cult ceremonies adduce any evidence that Legba is worshipped by these people. This is still

[73] *Ibid.*, pp. 150-151.
[74] *Ibid.*, pp. 101-103.
[75] *Ibid.*, Vol. II, pp. 109, 155.
[76] Averekete, the youngest child of the Dahomean Hevioso pantheon, is a female *vodun*, but appears as a male *vodun* for the Maranhão cult group. In Dahomey, Abe is believed to be the father of this god. The fact that Verekete is the youngest and most resourceful deity in this pantheon may perhaps be associated with the circumstance that Saint Benedict, the Catholic saint with whom he is identified, is familiarly called Bibi by the Dahomean Negroes, an appellation which is employed by a large segment of the Negroes of São Luiz.

more striking when consideration is given to the fact, established beyond any doubt, that not only is this being known in the interior, where African cult practices are much weaker, but that the Yoruban group worships Lebara, the Yoruban counterpart of the Dahomean trickster, about whom they have developed an elaborate complex of ideas and rituals. Yet cult initiates in the Dahomean house stated again and again that no sacrifices were made there to this spirit in earlier times and none are made now to keep him away since the *vodun* themselves see to this. This does not mean that the deity Lebara, worshipped in the Yoruban cult house is unknown to the Dahomean group, who, with the Yoruban group, believe him to be an evil spirit identified with the Devil. But this is as far as the members of the Dahomean group go in their discussion about Lebara.

The *vodun* are ranked by the Dahomean group according to age. Some of them are very old, like Sapata, chief of the Da family, or Sobo, "mother" of Kevioso, or Zomadonu. Zaka and Agongonu of the Davise "family" and Podibogi, son of Sapata, are said to be "mature." The other *vodun* are held to be somewhat younger, the youngest group, as previously seen, being the *tokhueni,* who are believed to be half-brothers, that is, not sons of the same father. Thus, Akuevi, Dosupe and Dese are children of Dosu Agaja and Dako is the son of Donu. The other *tokhueni,* Tosa and Tose, Jagoborosu, Apojevo, Bosu, Apoji and Nani, are believed to have been reared by Dadaho, the father of all the *vodun,* and serve as messengers between the *vodun* and the cult initiates[77] having the task of "opening the way" for their elders among the gods when there is a ceremony or a dance. In fulfilling this function, Tosa and Jagoborosu are believed to be "guides" and should come first, though in case no initiates vowed to them is present to act for them, Dako, who is an "adjutant" sees to it that the other *vodun* can enter and be worshipped.

In addition to the *vodun* and *tokhueni,* there are in the Dahomean house, as mentioned, child spirits, known by the Portuguese term *meninas* (little girls) or by a term of probable Dahomean origin, *tobosa.* They cause the *hunjai,* the cult members who have been duly initiated, to talk in a child-like manner and to play with dolls like children. Nine of these *meninas* are differentiated at the present time: Adagebe, Asadolebe, Afrovive, Torotoro, Asodovi, Homahuibe, Asanhabebe, Wherobe, and Sandolebe. Each is believed to be dominated by the male *vodun* by whom the woman cult initiate is usually possessed.

[77] This is also a Dahomean pattern according to which the gods can be reached only through a messenger. In Dahomey, Legba, the trickster, is the messenger of all gods and their spokesman (Herskovits, 1938, Vol. II, p. 223).

Let us now compare with the above deities those worshipped in the Yoruban house. Here the Dahomean term for deity, *vodun,* is often heard, though the Yoruban word *orisha* (*or orisa*)[78] is frequently used in songs. The gods worshipped by this group have Yoruban, Dahomean and Brazilian names. Interestingly enough, names of Yoruban derivation are few in number: Shango, Yemanja, Shapana, Ogun, Eowa, Osain, and Aduda.[79] The last two are rarely mentioned and have no cult initiates. Some of the Dahomean deities, Lisa, Loko and Bosa, are not only known, but have been actually incorporated into the worship of the group, which means that these deities have devotees in the Yoruban house. Nana-Buluku, whom the Dahomeans regard as the Creator,[80] is mentioned as Nana-Buruko in the Yoruban group though he is not included in any of the "families" of the Dahomean cult center. The *encantados* with *Brazilian* names are either conceived as nobles, some with such titles as prince, king and *dom,* or are caboclo gods, that is, Indian spirits. Of the nobles, those who have devotees are: King Kotelo, Servana, King Junko, Maria Alfa, Gama, Dom Luiz, Prince Viola, Rolo do Mar and Menino Fama, who fall in the same category as Dahomean and Yoruban deities, these being also said to be nobles. Only three Indian spirits have devotees: Caboclo Guerreiro, Caboclo Bahiano and Caboclo Tabajara. All the *encantados,* nobles and *cabocles,* are believed to live in the *encantaria,* a region at the bottom of the sea, and to belong to what the devotees call "lines." These "lines" are three in number: the Nago (Yoruban) line, the Taipa (Nupe) line and the *caboclo* or forest line.

In addition to retaining only a few aboriginal names of deities, the Yoruban cult group has failed to retain any considerable proportion of the beliefs concerning the organization of these deities, especially when compared to the Dahomean cult group. One does hear cult members speak of the "families" of the *vodun;* thus Shango, who is identified with the corresponding Thunder deity Bade of the Dahomeans, is said to have a large family, but strikingly enough, all its members are Dahomean: Loko, Verekete, Lisa, and Abe. Osain is held to belong to another "family," and Ogun to still another, neither of which, however, can be named.

Though few names of Yoruban gods have been maintained, the attributes of some of these deities are well known, and correspond to those of the same beings in Nigeria. Shango is recognized as having control over Thunder,

[78] Farrow, 1926, p. 34; Johnson, 1934, p. 60; and Bascom, 1944, p. 21.

[79] The names as well as the names of the other Yoruban deities can be found in such standard works on Yoruban cultures as those of Talbot, 1921, Vol. II, pp. 29-34, 37, 82, 93; of Johnson, 1934, pp. 26-39; Farrow, 1926, pp. 64-5; and Bascom, 1944, pp. 29-38.

[80] Herskovits, 1938, Vol. II, p. 101.

Yemanja over the waters, while Shapana, the Sapata of the Dahomean group, is known as the god who gives and takes away diseases of the skin. In addition to these beliefs, certain tales told of these deities by the older cult members are in the African pattern. The best known is about Shango, who is persecuted by Yemanja. He had had several children by different women, and left them with Yemanja to rear. Yemanja, however, followed him wherever he went, but disguised himself under different names so she could not find him: Bade, Abakuso and Gunoco, the latter being a Tapa (Nupe) name.[81] She finally catches up with him after a strenuous search, and marries him. In accordance with this myth, when there is a dance for the *vodun*, songs that refer to these episodes are sung, and the dancing of the devotees of these gods dramatize the episodes of the tale.

As has been previously stated, the Yoruban group have continued the tradition of the Yoruban-Dahomean trickster Lebara, though in modified form. It is to be noted that the other Yoruban designation for this deity, Eshu, is rarely encountered. However, while this trickster, in Nigeria and in Dahomey, is an amiable character, able to work evil but also a doer of good, for the São Luiz Yoruban group Lebara or Elebara is only malignant. "He is bad, we do not want to have business with him," they say, and feel that it is necessary to keep him away from their rites. "He likes to come to the dances," which makes it necessary to send him away before any dance is started. If a sacrifice is offered to a *vodun*, Lebara must first be "fed" so that, satisfied, he will not make trouble, such as causing a fight between dancers or in the audience, or spoiling the offering for the *vodun*. This is why he is worshipped before the other deities. A speckled cock is sacrificed to him, the blood caught in a dish and the meat roasted. Lebara is so feared that the utensils used to prepare this offering are employed exclusively for this purpose, and the persons engaged in the preparation of the sacrifice must keep away from others.

When we turn to our third category of cult centers, the Yoruban-derived houses, we find that most deities worshipped are *encantados* having Brazilian names: the names of Indian tribes, Tupi, Tupinambo; or *encantados* called *brancos* (white) or nobles, kings, princes or simply *dom*. Only a very few spirits have African designations. The African names that are most heard are Ogun, Verekete, Shapana and Bade; others less often encountered being Yemanja, Eowa and Shango. These latter may be mentioned by the cult heads, but play no role in the cult itself. This would seem to indicate that tendencies in the direction of the loss of African elements

---

[81] The Nupe have come under the influence of Islam and live north of the Yoruba (Nadel, 1942).

and the acceptance of Indian and European spirits already manifest in the Yoruban house have been carried farther in the Yoruban-derived cult centers.

The associates of these cult houses share with the Yoruban group the belief that the *encantados* live at the bottom of the sea—the *encantaria*—distributing themselves in various lines,[82] of which three are most often mentioned: Caboclo; African and Sea (*ondiná*). In addition to these, others are the Astral line, the *Surrupira* line, the "lower" line, and the line of the dead. The *Surrupira* line is named after the *caboclo* spirit Surrupira whose attributes are those of a trickster. Surrupira is believed to make a person who is possessed by him dance violently; he is also said to lure anyone he desires to punish into a thorny bush.[83] The line of the dead seems to be the result of the diffusion of Spiritualist ideas, now in process, and the mention of an Eshu line suggests that the name of the Yoruban trickster is at least known to persons who do not belong to the Yoruban cult center. Besides being called the "evil man" and being identified with the devil by some members of the Yoruban-derived cult houses, nothing else is said about Eshu by these persons.

The beliefs held by the Maranhão Negroes concerning the supernatural, some of which have been described above, cannot be understood without reference to the identity held to exist between the African gods and the saints of the Church. The character of these identifications, it should be pointed out, are marked by a great range of variation. By some, the saints are identified with the *encantados,* while others hold these spirits to be associated with the saints. Different concepts are encountered in the same center, held by the same person. At the Dahomean cult house, for example, the same person will state that a saint, in his capacity, as "a mystery," is a *vodun,* Saint Barbara, for example, being a saint in heaven, but as "a mystery" is called Sobo. He will then go on to explain that the saints are different from the *vodun,* that the *vodun* are merely spirits born on the feast days of the saints, who thus become their spokesmen and protectors. Sobo is believed to have been born on the feast day of Saint Barbara; or it

---

[82] Whether the "line" concept was transmitted by the Yoruban cult group to the Yoruban-derived or vice versa, it was not possible to verify. As to its origin, it is suggested here that it is perhaps Angolan-derived, since it is well known in Rio de Janeiro in the Angolan-derived cult centers (Ramos, 1940, pp. 124, 133) and it is not used in the Dahomean or Yoruban centers of worship anywhere else.

[83] Surrupira is another form of Curupira, an Indian deity. Among Tupi tribes he is the deity who protects the forests, punishing those who cut down a tree by making them lose their way in the bush (Magalhaes, 1876, pp. 138-139).

will be said that Dosu, who is thought of as a poet, and is always found on horseback, was born on the day devoted to Saint George, who is his protector. Tosa and Tose, who are twins, are logically identified with the twin saints Comas and Damien.

As elsewhere in the New World,[84] these identifications are, in the main, based on the recognition of similar qualities possessed by the African deities and the Catholic saints. Thus, in the Dahomean house, Sobo, mother of the Thunder god Kevioso is identified with Saint Barbara because Catholic theology holds that she protects her devotees from thunder. Sapata, the Dahomean Earth-god who punishes with skin disease, is identified with Saint Lazarus, the saint of small-pox. The Dahomean god Dosu obviously shares his trait of horsemanship with Saint George, the dragon-killer, who is his counterpart. And Nae or Maedona is identified with Our Lady, while Jesus Christ, God and the Holy Ghost, as we have previously seen, are given the title Evo-Vodun, i.e. they who are above all other *vodun*.

Identification between saints and African deities is greater in the Yoru--ban cult house than elsewhere and a longer list of identifications can be obtained there than among the Dahomean group. Those who belong to the Yoruban group say that the saints receive their *vodun* names when they "come down" and possess a cult initiate; that the saint is the same as the *vodun*, the former being honored as the latter when he possesses a cult member. The following identifications are made:

Shango	St. Peter
Yemanja	Our Lady of Good Parturition
Shapana	St. Sebastian
Ogun	St. John
Osain	St. Francis
Eowa	Our Lady of Conception
Nana Buroko	St. Rita
Lisa	St. Paul

In the Yoruban-derived cult houses, where, as has been explained, the names of only a few African deities are heard, Ogun, Verekete, Shapana and Bade, these beings are not themselves believed to possess cult initiates, but they are, nevertheless, identified with the Catholic saints in the manner of the Yoruban cult group. In addition, members of both the Yoruban and Yoruban-derived cult houses believe that the worship of the *encantados* is sponsored by Saint Barbara, who is said by some members of the Yoruban-derived cult houses to have been the founder of the *terreiros de mina* everywhere, and to have installed Verekete as her "delegate" to guide the ceremonies.

[84] Herskovits, 1937 *b*, pp. 635, 643.

In both the Dahomean and Yoruban houses, the African gods have more than one name, the Dahomean group in particular having preserved the tradition of giving "praise names" to their deities. Podibogi, for instance, receives the following name: Dada-Misu-Cohoe-Jeko-Da-Mede-Metonji-Lakaba-Lube-Adonovi-Vipenhon-Sadono-Abrogevi-Boi-Hanhi-Hae-Hanshi. Agongonu is praised as Savalu-Hoso-Lise-Ahoso-Hompeze-Tripapa-Duheme. In the Yoruban house, Shango is known by the names of Kevioso and Bade, of Dahomean derivation, and as Abakuso and Gunoco, which are, respectively, a Yoruban praise name for Shango, and a Nupe-derived designation. Ogun is called, in accordance with the various ways in which he manifests himself, Ogun ota, Ogun ona, Ogun *moço* (the young Ogun) and Ogun *velho* (the old Ogun), these being retentions of the Yoruban traditions of ascribing different "qualities" to a deity.[85]

The explanations of cult members, when asked why their deities have several names, are revealing of their psychology in these matters. Thus, members of the two "orthodox" houses pointed out that saints can also have different appellations. "Doesn't Our Lady," they said, "have several names, too. Our Lady of Glory, Our Lady of Pity, Our Lady of Conception and so forth?" And just as each of these names, it was indicated, symbolizes "one of her miracles," the same is true of the corresponding *vodun*. Thus, it is to be seen how the process of identification has been facilitated, here as elsewhere in the New World, by similarities in African and Catholic concepts of supernatural beings, and how the recognition of these resemblances have given psychological validity to the resulting syncretisms.

Caboclo spirits (those which represent Indian deities) are not identified with saints. "*Caboclo* is not saint," it is said. Though it is recognized that like the saints, they help and protect human beings. On the other hand, many of the spirits considered nobles or Whites, are said to be the equivalent of the saints whose names they bear, that is, Dom Sebastian is equated with St. Sebastian, Barbara with St. Barbara, Dom John with St. John. Since like the African and *caboclo* gods, they "come down" to dance in the persons of their devotees, it would seem that the new spirits thus created have developed in accordance with both Catholic and African patterns, as would be expected. The Catholic pattern is represented by the use of the names of saints, the phenomenon of possession they manifest is in accordance with the African pattern.

Cult rituals. Worship of the *encantados* closely follows African patterns only in the two "orthodox" houses. Of these two, the Dahomean cult house shows purer African forms of ritual than the Yoruban, while the other houses,

[85] Talbot, 1926, Vol. II, p. 29.

as is to be inferred from the preceding discussion, tend to manifest non-African elements in still greater measure. In the Dahomean cult house, the songs and drum rhythms which accompany the dances are pure African, as are the words to the songs, which are in Fō, the language of Dahomey. On the other hand, in the Yoruban center, the words to songs are either Nago, the language of the Yoruba, in mixed Nago and Portuguese, or in Portuguese. In the Yoruban-derived cult groups only relatively few songs are in Nago, and many of these, according to members of the Yoruban cult groups, are not sung correctly.

In all centers, however, syncretisms between Catholic and African elements are to be observed in ritual, as they are in respect to belief. Though dances may be held any time except during Lent, they generally take place on the feast days of certain Catholic saints, notably those of St. Barbara, Our Lady of Conception, St. Sebastian, St. John and St. Benedict. Christmas and New Year are also occasions for important ceremonies in most houses, the annual festivals occurring in all cult houses in December and January, especially in the Yoruban and in the Dahomean centers where sacrifices are then offered to the *vodun*. But it is to be understood that in these two houses, a dance to honor a saint always mean honoring the African deity with which he is identified.

At the beginning of an important dance, a *ladainha* is held in a room of the cult center which has a sanctuary or an improvised altar. On this are placed images of the saints. The *ladainha*, as we have seen, is a series of church prayers and hymns to honor a saint and seek his protection. In the Dahomean house, a most interesting syncretism is to be observed in regard to the *ladainhas*, for here the cult initiates, possessed by African gods, attend these rites dressed in the costumes of their respective deities. While the prayers are recited they remain silent, standing near the sanctuary or improvised altar, but when these are over, the possessed cult initiates who, it must be remembered, are for the cult group the *vodun* themselves, in their turn, sing a "*ladainha*" in the African language, Fō, honoring the *vodun* whose feast day is being celebrated. In other centers, the initiates, dressed in the regalia of the gods (though not possessed by them), sing only the Catholic *ladainha*.

At a dance in the Dahomean cult house, the musical accompaniment ordinarily composed of three male drummers, plus one woman playing a iron gong and three or more women playing rattles. The drums are single headed, hollow-log instruments of the African type; the skin of each drum is attached to its body by pegs. All of them are called by Dahomean names.

[86] Information given by M. J. Herskovits.

The biggest is the *hun*, a word from which derives the term by which the the drummers are known to the cult group, *hunto*; *hunto*-chief is the name of the drummer who plays the *hun*. The drum of average size is called *gunpli* and the name *hunpli* is given to the smallest. Wooden drumsticks are called *agidavi*, as in Dahomey. Two are used for the small and average size drums, but only one is used on the *hun*, its head and its body being beaten by the drummer. The iron, a very important instrument, which sets the basic rhythm, is called *ga*, as mentioned before, the woman who plays it being called *gato*. *Shekere* is the African word by which the rattles are designated, but the Portuguese word *cabaça* (calabash) is also used. The players are seated while playing.

As the musical accompaniment begins its rhythms, the cult initiates seat themselves on a bench at the side of the women who are playing the rattles and join them and the woman who plays the iron in singing the songs which call the gods. To bring the spirits to their heads the cult initiates gently rub one hand against the other. When possession ensues, they get to their feet and begin to dance, and each is offered a white cloth to tie around the waist or about the breasts. These cloths indicate that the personalities of the women have been displaced by the gods, so that from that moment on they are the *vodun* themselves, and are to be treated accordingly. Thus, when a possessed person is to be offered a cloth, an assistant kneels and respectfully proffers it to the deity. After the women sitting on the bench are possessed, the music stops for about twenty minutes or half an hour while the initiates are taken to different rooms inside the house and dressed in the ceremonial regalia of the *vodun*. A sign is then given to the players to resume playing, whereupon the devotees, under possession and in costume, return to the dancing space in order of precedence, the *tokhueni* coming first, followed by the *vodun* belonging to the "family" of Danbira, then those of the Davise group, and finally the ones headed by Kevioso. In each "family," in turn, the order of the *vodun* follows the criterion of age, the youngest being first. The possessed cult initiates now dance for two or three hours, each *vodun* in turn taking intervals of rest during which a possessed person will speak with other members of the house, embracing and blessing them.

The order in which the songs are sung varies in accordance with the deity who is being celebrated, but the Adajibe song comes first on all occasions, since it calls all the gods:

> Adajibe Bodo Daeme,
> Ahole Bodo Daeme,
> Emimaho pa pa, be.[87]

[87] These verses are repeated several times.

Possessions by the *vodun* come as the songs sacred to each are sung. However, if these do not ensue, another song to call the gods is tried:

> Nyolo vodun
> Huanlebi iobono jawa
> E eiolo Zomadonu enozon
> Vodono jawa.

But should this song not bring them, then the "strongest" of all,[88] that it is believed cannot fail to induce the desired possessions, is heard:

> Bunholoe majohã
> Bunholoe anawa,
> Ajonovekinin kanhã
> Bunholoe anawa
> Bunholoe najohã
> Bunholoe anawa.

In the normal course of events, however, possessions are brought on as the songs for each "family" of *vodun* are sung, which makes unnecessary the last two of these songs. The Adajibe is immediately followed by songs for the *tokhueni*, since, as previously mentioned, these deities are supposed to "open the way" for the other *vodun*. It sometimes happens, however, that those who worship the *tokhueni* only become possessed after the cult initiates who are devotees of the older *vodun* are possessed by their gods. Should this happen, those who "belong" to the *tokhueni* sing a song excusing themselves—that is, the deities—for their late arrival. This song, like those previously given, is in Fō:

> Deshe nolomie
> Idoselo melode
> Deshe nolomie
> Unhweso
> Iabome
> Deshe nolomie.

In accordance with the rules of precedence, the last initiates to be possessed are those who worship the Kevioso deities. But the order of songs when those under possession, dressed as the gods, return from the inside of the house to the dancing space is somewhat different, in that the first songs are in honor of the *vodun* whose feast day is being celebrated. But after these, the songs are sung in their customary sequence.

---

[88] These songs are the equivalents of the drum rhythms that bring on possessions in the Bahian cult houses, rhythms termed the *adahun*. Cf. Ramos, 1940, p. 241.

The tempo of the music varies with the deities for whom it is being played. For the *tokhueni,* who are young, it is fast, and those possessed by these spirits dance with quick steps. For the "families" of Davise and Danbira, whose members are more mature, the music is slower at the beginning, though from the middle towards the end it is accelerated, reaching its climax with a fast tempo. The dancing of these possessed by either Davise or Danbira consists of measured, simple steps when the time is slow—the dancer shifting from one foot to another—but when the rhythm becomes rapid, the choreography is more complex and the dance much more dynamic. Those possessed by the oldest *vodun,* Zomadonu, Zaka, Agongonu, Dosu, Podibogi and Ajauto de Aladano, carry staffs as symbols of their old age and their high status. Drum rhythms for Kevioso, the god of Thunder, are loud and fast, and the associated dance is performed in a lively manner. As the rhythms of each pantheon are sounded, its members dance in front of the drums, facing them, while the *vodun* of the other "families" stand in the back part of the dancing space watching the others dance or following the rhythm quietly without moving. Now and then all the *vodun* bow to the drums thus recognizing their importance as the means by which they have been brought to the heads of their worshippers.

When it is time to end the dance, the cult head gives a sign to the drummers and to the *gato,* the person who plays the iron gong, to sound the proper rhythms of dismissal. The musicians rise and so do the members of the audience while this song is being sung, and all the possessed cult initiates dance. Then everyone is seated, and while the drums continue playing the "deities" form in two lines, one long one in which the *tokhueni* come followed by Danbira and Davise, the other composed only of the members of the Kevioso "family." The first group leave the dancing space first, but they immediately return to take away the Kevioso "deities," who they must urge to stop dancing, and to come away with the other *vodun.* When the former finally agree, all the "gods" then leave and the dance ends. In their exit, the *vodun* do not always observe the same order of precedence, except that the three oldest members of the Davise "family," Zomadonu, Zaka and Agongonu always end the procession, Zomadonu being the last. And as each *vodun* departs, he turns and bows in the direction of the drums, thus again paying them his respect. After the public rite is over, the "gods" talk among themselves or to their associates, receiving thanks for aid given their devotees or being asked for advice or favors. One or two hours later, the *vodun* are ritualistically sent away, and the cult initiates become themselves once more.

The dance just described is held three successive nights, usually Saturdays, Sundays and Mondays. This is an ordinary dance to worship the *vodun*. In addition to such dances, there are those held especially at the end of one year and beginning of the other—the annual festivals which involve the sacrifice of chickens or other animals. These rites loom large in the worship of the *vodun*. When a sacrifice is going to be offered to a deity, the cult initiates receive their *vodun* in the room (*pegi*) where the objects sacred to the gods are placed; that is, possession occurs there instead of in the dancing space. This occurs during the ceremony called *zãdro* already previously mentioned, which is usually held late in the evening at ten or eleven o'clock of the first night of the three-day dance series. The cult initiates sit on the floor on a mat, grouped in accordance with the "family" of the deities to whom they "belong." They clap their hands and sing songs calling the *vodun* to possess them, while the *gato* and two or three women who play the rattles stand up and play their instruments, the iron and the rattles. The drummers also attend this ceremony but do not play since their instruments are left in the veranda where the dance is usually held. The order in which the songs are sung indicates the order in which possession occurs; first, the *tokhueni*, then Davise, then Danbira, finally Kevioso. As this ceremony, which takes about half an hour, ends, the possessed women, dressed in clean white clothes, go to the dancing space, and then dance for a period of approximately one hour so that the dance will be ended at about half past midnight. The gods are then ritualistically sent away, and the cult initiates usually sleep a little, though some may remain awake and engage in conversation.

At day-break, the ceremony called *nahunū*, at which the sacrifices are offered to the deity in the *pegi* takes place. The cult initiates gather there again. The chief drummer is in charge of the killing of the animals when the *vodunsi* are once more possessed by their respective gods. After the offering of the blood of the animals to the deities, the flesh is cooked and the special dishes which are prepared are taken to the *pegi* where they are presented to the *vodun*. In the late afternoon these dishes are taken out and are then distributed among the cult initiates and other members of the group. On the night of that day and the following, dances are held to especially honor the *vodun* for whom the sacrifices were offered. Thus, as on the previous nights, the first songs which are sung in the dancing space are those of this deity, the order after these being the customary one.

These two ceremonies, *zãdro* and *nahunū*, are important elements in the obligations of the cult members to the deities they worship, and it is actually stated by the cult initiates that it is an *obrigacão* (an obligation) to hold them. And though sacrifices are most often made at the end of the year when the annual festivities for the *vodun* are held, they can begin at any time of the year a cult initiate wishes to give an offering to her god, or is instructed by the deity to do so.

In the Yoruban-derived cult houses, two double-headed European-type drums called *abata* are played horizontally on tripod-like structures, the drummers being called *abataseiros*. This is different from the African custom of using three or more drums. An iron gong and rattles are the other instruments played as in the Dahomean house. The Yoruban name *agogo* serves to designate the iron gong, while the terms *shekere* and *cabaça*, used by the Dahomean group to designate the rattles, serve the same purpose in the Yoruban and the Yoruban-derived cult centers. In these centers, when the music begins, the dancers enter in line already dressed as the *encantados*. They first dance facing the drums, forming two or three or four rows of four or five dancers each, later also circling the dancing space in counter clockwise direction.

In the Yoruban center, there is more variation of rhythms and styles of dancing than in the Yoruban-derived cult houses, where only two basic styles generally known under the terms *dobrado* and *corrido,* are to be found. The *corrido* style of drumming is the simpler of the two: it consists of short almost unsyncopated rhythmic patterns repeated over and over again at a rapid tempo. The *dobrado,* on the other hand, while it may be slower in tempo, calls for much more skill and artistry on the part of the drummer, since the "open" rhythmic figures, highly syncopated and stressing the "off-beat" often last longer than the melodic phrases with which they are associated, so that there is frequently no appearance of repetition at all in the drumming. After the music has been playing for ten to twenty minutes or more, and possession comes to each dancer, a white cloth is tied about the body as in the Dahomean house. In some of the Yoruban-derived centers, where Indian deities play an important role, however, the possessed devotees wear a large kerchief on one shoulder, an *espada,* as it is called, and bead necklaces called *incruzo,* hang across both shoulders and to the waist.

As among the Dahomean group, the songs in the Yoruban house follow a set order. To open the ceremony, as the women, in line, enter the dancing space, they sing to Lebara, though they are unaware of the purpose of this opening song and of the tradition of making an offering to this being before the other deities are called for worship:

> Imbarabo Mojuba,
> Imbarabo Mojuba,
> Omadeko Jibabo,

Ale Mojuba,
O Lebara Bonimi.[89]

The song which follows is for Ogun, a type of which the following is one
example:

Ogun nosho
Ogun nosho
Ashae, shae
Ogun o.
Ogun de Tabiode,
Jara Jojo Ogunde.
E do Ogun Naba,
Ogun o.
E de Ogun Naba,
Ogun o.

Then follow songs for Shango, Yemanja, Nana Buruko, Shapana, Osain,
Obaila, Misa, Loko, Eowa, and Verekete in this order. One or two songs are
sung for each but Shango is accorded at least six because he is the "master
of the house" (*dono da casa*). The following is one of his songs:

E Mije, Mije,
Ko Koko;
E Mije, Mije,
Ko Antã;
Ajalekun beleku Kurimã,
E Kurimã, e Kurimã,
Akompanie.

As in the Dahomean cult center, if possession by the *vodun* does not
come, a song to call the gods is sung:

Kalulu, Kalulu,
Ae Kalulu;
O Boni Kalulu
Ae Kalulu;
Kalumbe, Kalimbeawo
Ae Kalimbeawo.

The songs for the Yoruban deities mentioned above are those for the
Nago "line." They are followed by a few others, not more than five, for
deities of the Taipa (Tapa, i.e., Nupe) "line." The words to these songs also
seem to be in Nago. The following is for the *encantado* named Zezinho:

[89] A similar song opens the ceremonies in the cult houses in Bahia, and in
Port-of-Prince (Trinidad), where they were recorded by Dr. M. J. Herskovits.

Manza, Manza
Obesi Mawe
Manza Orisa
Manza, Manza,
Obesi Mawe.

Then come songs for the "line of the forest" (*linha da mata*), having words either in Nago, in mixed Portuguese-Nago or in Portuguese. Examples of those words are in Nago-Portuguese:

1.

E Mulukã, Mulukã,	E Mulukã, Mulukã,
E Mulukã Jalo;	E Mulukã, Jalo
Oia a moça, vem ve	Come and see the young lady,
E Mulukã Jalo	E Mulukã Jalo.

2.

Bada de Oio,[90]	Bada from Oio
É de Jão, Jõ Tirijão;	Is John, John Tirijão;
O Bade Kevioso,	Bade Kevioso
É de Jão, Jão Tirijão	Is John, John Tirijão;
Kimire miko bafeu,	Kimire miko bafeu
É de Jão, Jão Tirijão.	Is John, John Tirijão.

The Muluka song is not dedicated to any deity in particular; the second is sung for Bade. The following have Portuguese words:

1.

Eu sou balanco do má	I am the movement of the waves
Eu vim da Mina Gerá;	I come from Minas Gerais;
Meu pai foi quem me mandô	My father it was who sent me,
Eu vim da Mina Gerá	I come from Minas Gerais.

2.

Veio do ceu, Manja	Manja has come from heaven,
Veio do ceu	She has come from heaven.
Senhora Mãe,	Lady Mother
Veio do ceu.	Has come from heaven
Veio do ceu, Manja	Manja has come from heaven,
Veio do ceu,	She has come from heaven
Senhor meu Pai	My Lord Father
Veio do ceu.	Has come from heaven.

The last song honors Yemanja.

In some of the Yoruban-derived cult centers, though the first song is the one already cited which begins with the word *Imbarabo* and a few that fol-

[90] Name of a city in Nigeria.

low also have Nago words, Portuguese words are added to the Nago in most of the others. In some of these houses, no Nago songs are sung at all, the first ones being greetings to the cult house itself rather than to the gods:

1.

Salvá, Salvá,	I have come to praise him,
Eu vim salvá aqui;	To praise, to praise;
Salvá, senhor meu Pai,	I come to praise my father
Eu vim salvá aqui.	I come to praise him here.

2.

Ae eu vim salvá,	I have come to praise
Terreiro novo de meu Pai	My father's new *terreiro*.
Eu vim salvá.	I come to praise it.

These are followed by songs in honor of Saint Barbara, who is everywhere "chief" of the *terreiros do mina*, and of Verekete (Saint Benedict) appointed by Saint Barbara to act as her delegate, or the "guide" in the ceremonies of these cult houses. These songs are of the following type:

1.

Minha divina Santa Barbara	My Blessed Saint Barbara,
Ó Senhora minha;	My Lady;
Minha divina Santa Barbara	My Blessed Saint Barbara,
Venha ver seu mundo.	Come and see your world.

2.

Verekete é reis,	Verekete is king,
Croado no mar;	He was crowned in the sea;
Croou, croou, croou,	He was crowned, he was crowned
Croado no mar.	He was crowned in the sea.

Dom John is an *encantado* greatly esteemed, and many songs are sung for him:

1.

Ai Dom João, Dom João	O Dom John, Dom John
É rei de Mina.	Is King of Mina
Ai Dom João, Dom João	Dom John, Dom John
É rei mineiro.	Is king of the men of Mina.

2.

Dom João Soeira,	Dom John Soeira,
Cavaleiro do mar,	Horseman of the sea,
Ó sela teu cavalo, Soeira,	Saddle your horse, Soeira,
Vamos passear.	Let us be off.

Songs for the *caboclo* spirits are also popular:

1.

Eu sou caboclo,	I am *caboclo*
Eu vim da India, meu pai	I come from India, father,
Eu sou caboclo,	I am *caboclo*.

Eu vim da India, meu pai;	I come from India, father,
Me chamo Mariano,	My name is Mariano,
Moro nas onda do mar.	And I live on the waves of the sea.

2.

Tenho a minha lança,	I have my spear,
Tenho a minha tamaranda,	I have my club;
Tenho o meu arco	I have my bow,
A minha flexa nao me engana.	And my arrow goes straight.

3.

Imba fóra, Surrupira,	Get out, Surrupira,
Imba fóra, Guerreiro,	Get out, Warrior,
Imba fóra, Surrupira,	Get out, Surrupira,
Imba fóra, Guerreiro.	Get out, Warrior.

Dancing in the houses situated near the city, that is, in the Dahomean and the Yoruban centers and one Yoruban-derived house, must stop soon after midnight by police order. Elsewhere, however, dancing sometimes continues until dawn. In the Yoruban house, those who are possessed form in line to leave the dancing space. In the other houses, the dancers send their spirits away ritualistically before the dance is over, and only a few possessed persons are on the floor as the ceremony ends.

Though the phenomenon of possession is fundamentally the same in all cult groups, certain variations can easily be noted by the observer. In the two "orthodox" centers, especially the Dahomean, it is restrained and seems to be induced in accordance with well-defined patterns, but most often it would be difficult to judge if a person is experiencing the state of possession or not, for only the white cloth tied about the individual to whom the god has come would indicate this. In most of the Yoruban-derived cult houses, however, possession occurs with signs of extreme violence, the women whirling and dancing in a very rapid tempo. Here it seems to be a much more spontaneous phenomenon, controlled by fewer rules than in the "orthodox" houses, this being a reflex of the relaxation of the patterns of worship found in the Dahomean and, to a lesser degree, in the Yoruban center. But in no cult houses in the city can signs of motor behavior so characteristic of African possession be observed as in the interior.

The *vodun* are ritualistically sent away in the private room in a manner that varies only slightly from one center to another. The possessed person, or persons, lay down on a mat on the floor, or on a bed, in the *pegi* or another inside room, and are then entirely covered by one of the possessed women or by the cult head, with the white cloth that was tied around their bodies, or any other white cloth. Then, as the cloth is lifted, the deity is supposed to depart and possession ends.

In the Dahomean house, the same person behaves differently when possessed by a *vodun* and by the type of spirit called *tobosa,* conceived to be that of a child. Possession of the *tobosa* takes place only three times a year, at New Year's, at Carnival time, and in June during the festivals for Saint John. In each of these occasions a *hunjai,* that is, a cult initiate who is possessed by a *tobosa,* experiences this state for several days in succession, several hours each day. If there is a dance on any of these days, however, after the *tobosa* has withdrawn, the *hunjai* becomes possessed by her *vodun,* when her behavior becomes entirely different from what it was when she was possessed by the *tobosa.* As a *vodun,* the possessed person is grave and fatherly. As *tobosa,* however, she speaks and behaves as a child of three or four years, playing with dolls, making necklaces of beads, curious and bashful. This special state of possession can be compared to that which is observed in Bahia[91] or in Port of Spain, Trinidad,[92] where possession by a deity is followed by a playful childlike mood—termed *ere* in Bahia and *weri* in Port of Spain—before the initiate becomes his or her old self again. In Maranhão, however, the *tobosa* form of possession, experienced only in the Dahomean house, precedes rather than follows the state of possession by an adult deity, and nowhere in São Luiz cult houses was a transitional playful form of possession or semi-possession observed between full possession and usual behavior.

In addition to the possession dances, other ceremonies of the cult houses may be considered. The baptism of new musical instruments, drums, iron, rattles, is everywhere important,[93] for it is believed that "heathen" instruments, i.e. unbaptized ones, can bring on possession by evil spirits. In baptizing a drum, a "priest," either a man or a woman possessed by a male *encantado,* recites the church baptismal formulae, giving the drum its name in the presence of a godfather and a godmother previously chosen by the priestess or friends of the cult house. The godfather stands at one side, holding in his hand a lighted candle which is afterwards left in front of the drum, or at the altar where the ceremony is performed.

Although it is believed in the two "orthodox" houses that drums must be fed, that is, offerings of food given them, the last ceremony of this type held in the Dahomean house took place about ten years ago. At that time a cock, a chicken and some pigeons were killed, their blood sprinkled over the drums, and the cooked fowl were deposited with their food in front of the

---

[91] Herskovits, M. J. and F. S., 1943, pp. 278-279; Landes, 1940, p. 267.

[92] Observation made by the author in September, 1944, during attendance at a dance in one of the cult houses of the African-derived Shango sect.

[93] Herskovits, 1937, pp. 275-277; 1944, p. 484.

drums for a time, being later distributed to the cult initiates and other cult members. In the Yoruban house, although a special ceremony like the above is not held, cult initiates say that drums "eat" whenever a sacrifice is offered to a *vodun*.

A dance called the *tambor de pagamento* is held to reward the musicians who have played for the *vodun* on the occasion of the regular rituals of the cult house, and to thank them for their work. This dance is not held except in the two orthodox houses, and not every year there. At the Dahomean house, it is held outside in the yard, where benches are placed on both sides of the drums so that a large space is left for the *vodun* to dance. As the music begins, the initiates in line, and dancing, enter the space from inside the house. The *tokhueni* come in front, holding the gifts to be given the musicians, followed by the *vodun* grouped in "families" in the customary order. After some minutes of beautiful dancing to a special song, the *tokhueni* give to each musician a gift (a shirt, a handkerchief, a bottle of wine, a small amount of money). The words of this song are:

> Unze bojaa awe
> Unze ebo.
> Unze bojaa awe
> Kuhun levi obo.
>
> Unze bojaa awe
> Unze ebo.
>
> Unze bojaa awe
> Dada-Misu-Huelo.
>
> Unze bojaa awe
> Unze ebo.
> Unze bojaa awe
> Dako-Dako-Donu.
>
> Unze bojaa awe
> Unze ebo
> Azu apregudo.
>
> Unze bojaa awe
> Unze ebo
> Agaja-Masu-Hondo.
>
> Unze bojaa awe
> Unze ebo.
> Bade-Jodu-Sobo

    Unze bojaa awe
    Unze ebo.
    Loko-Loko-Alikina
    Unze bojaa awe
    Unze ebo.

After this, the rite continues in the manner of ordinary dances already described.

In the Yoruban house, this dance is held at the back of the house, but, as in the case of other ceremonies, it is not as impressive as at the Dahomean center. Here, too, however, a special song for the occasion is sung, its words being:

Sobo, no mocambo,   Sobo, in her hut
Tem dinheiro.   Has money.
Bade, no mocambo,   Bade, in his hut
Tem dinheiro.   Has money.

As the initiates sing, they give gifts of the same nature as the above to the musicians, and distribute coins among the spectators whom they want to distinguish with their favors.

Our discussion of public ceremonies should not be ended without mention of a ceremony, held only at the Dahomean house, termed the "dinner for dogs" that occurs January twentieth of each year for the feast day of Saint Sebastian, a day on which Saint Lazarus identified with the African deity Sapata is also feasted. In Catholic theology Saint Lazarus is the protector of dogs. On the afternoon of his day, the cult members meet at the dancing space. Several dishes with food are placed on the floor, and the children between five and eight years of age, of cult initiates, musicians and cult associates, sit in front of them, each child with a dog at his side, to whom he gives of the various kinds of food as he eats. During this time, cult initiates under possession, dressed in the accoutrements of the gods walk about the children singing in Fō, honoring both Saint Lazarus and Sapata.

In addition to the ceremonies that can be witnessed by the public, there are many esoteric rites, especially in the two orthodox houses, which involve the sacrifices of animals and are held in the sanctuary. They may be attended only by cult initiates and other qualified cult members, such as drummers. In the Dahomean house, goats, chickens, cocks and pigeons are the animals most often sacrificed. Of these, the goat is by far the most important, because the "sacrifice of a four-footed animal is worth more to the "deity" than that of "an animal with two feet." When chickens or cocks are killed, their blood is merely poured over the stones, but in the case of a sheep or goat, its blood is allowed to coagulate and then cooked, when it constitutes a dish called *huesa* that is carried inside the *pegi* on a plate and offered to the *vodun*. This dish and dishes prepared with the meat of fowl which are offered the *vodun* in the *pegi* are merely placed before the shrine of the gods for a time, after which they are brought out and served to the cult house members.

The dishes prepared for the *vodun*, which are later eaten by the cult members are not only African in character, but have Dahomean names: *Agrala*, toasted chicken cooked with palm oil and rice flour; *amio*, chicken boiled with palm oil and rice flour; *cariru*, chicken made with okra and palm oil; *abobo*, beans prepared with palm oil; *amio*, dried shrimps with rice flour *acarage*, little cakes made of bean meal with palm oil; and *alua*, a drink made with corn and ginger. In the Yoruban house, as far as could be determined, the most common sacrifices are: *alua, cariru* and *acarage*. The name *amala*, given in Bahia as a food offering to an African deity,[94] is applied by the Yoruban cult group to a dish of *cariru* and *acarage* which may be offered both to the deities and to the drums. In the few other houses where offerings are made to the *encantados, cariru* and *alua* are the two most often used for the purpose. In all places, the sacrifices are eventually eaten by cult members.

In the Dahomean house, all the *vodun* accept chicken and goat sacrifices, but Sapata "eats" only pigeons, "Angola chickens," and popcorn. If there is an epidemic of skin disease, popcorn is offered him inside the house. The Yoruban group follows a similar pattern, although sacrifices occur less frequently. They appease Shapana, the deity in Yoruban belief which corresponds to the Dahomean Sapata, by offering him beans and corn, which they spread out in different parts of the city.

The actual killing of the animals (*matança*) is done by the chief drummer, with the help of his colleagues. In the Dahomean house, the *vodunsi* are possessed by their respective gods when an animal is being sacrificed, generally at Christmas, on New Year's Eve, Holy Saturday and on Saint Peter's day. In the Yoruban and other houses, general sacrifices are offered on New Year's Day, or on the days of either Saint Barbara or Saint Sebastian, but a cult initiate can make an offering at any time of the year if it is necessary to appease a god or to ask for his protection.

Magical practices. Let us now consider the complex of magical beliefs and practices which, paralleling what is found in the interior, is present in São Luiz as an integral part of the system of belief of a considerable number of Negroes, both members and non-members of the Afro-Brazilian cult groups. We have seen that an Indian magical tradition called pagelança or *cura* (healing) is an important feature of Negro culture in São Luiz. Afri-

---

[94] The name used there is *omala* (Ramos, 1940, p. 63).

can and European magical ideas and practices are also found there, not only those peculiar to each area but, as in the case of the belief in the "evil eye" and the tradition of the use of charms, beliefs that can be traced to Africa as well as to Europe.[95] This means that these beliefs have amalgamated and reinforced each other, a process identical to that which occurred in the field of religion, as previously seen.

Magic for the São Luiz Negro can be good or bad. The evil eye is the mildest form of the latter, though it is also believed that a single look of admiration by anyone can produce harmful consequences to the person or object being admired, this being the reason for the use of the magical expression "*figa, benza* Deus" when someone for instance praises a child. A person with the evil eye, however, need merely stare at another to cause the latter to feel tired and sleepy or even fall ill. Frequently, possession of the evil eye is unknown even to the person who owns it. The evil eye is generally considered a purposeful form of black magic, used to harm an enemy, a rival or a person who has aroused one's envy. To combat it, in either of its two forms, one who is believed to have been injured by it seeks someone who knows the prayers that must be said to ward off any harmful consequences.

The following prayer is especially used against the evil eye:

Dina pariu Ana,	Dina gave birth to Anne,
Ana pariu Maria	Anne gave birth to Mary,
Maria pariu Jesus;	Mary gave birth to Jesus;
Joana[96]	Joana
Que tu tem?	What is the matter with you?
Quebranto, mofina,	Are you bewitched?
Espanto, mau olhado?	What do you fear?
Dos olhos excomungado	The eye that was excommunicated
Deitaram pelo mar sagrado	Held in the sacred sea?
Se com dois te botaram,	If you have been bewitched by two (beings),
Com treis eu te tiro	I will cure you with three;
Com as treis divinas pessoa	The Divine Three
Da Santissima Trinidade;	Of the Holy Trinity;
Deus, Pai, Deus Filho	God Father, God Son,
Deus Espirito Santo. Amen	God Holy Ghost, Amen.

Men and women frequently wear carved charms in the shape of a clenched

[95] "Le regard est considéré par tous les gens de l'Ouest Africain comme une puissance qui peut être tantôt bonne et bienfaisante, tantot hostile et redoutable. Le mauvais oeil est connu de tous au Soudan et redouté par bien de gens" (Tauxier, 1927, pp. 21-22).

[96] Proper name of person who has been injured.

hand, the *figa*, the origin of which goes back to medieval Europe, to protect them from the evil eye.

Mention of the *figa* charm brings up the subject of charms which are used by some people to cure diseases or to bring good luck. Children commonly carry them to bring good luck and to avoid pain at the appearance of permanent teeth. The charm, which is usually a crocodile tooth, or a donkey's hair, is kept in a little sack suspended from the person's neck.

Black magic is generally known by the Portuguese terms *coisa feita*, *feitiço* and *porcaria* as in the interior, and by the term *coioio*, the latter of indeterminate origin. Black magic can cause greater damage than the evil eye. Disease and misfortune in economic ventures are often attributed to *coioio*. In love affairs, the possibility of black magic is always taken into account. To put someone under the magical spell, one has to have a piece of clothing the person wears, or to use special "prayers," or to make a toad swallow scales from a fish the person ate: in the last case, it is believed that the victim will die of an obstruction of the trachea. A practitioner of black magic can also do harm to a person if he has as much as a single hair of the victim. Responsibility for damage caused by black magic is ascribed to a rival, an enemy or an envious person, although, as happens in cases of sorcery, the sorcerer is almost never singled out. The latter may be either a layman or a professional practitioner who is paid for such a purpose. It is indicated that the *pagés* or *curadores* (healers) who practice curative magic are also engaged in black magic, a belief which finds expression in the following statement: "Those who free you from it (black magic) also make it," a belief widely spread throughout the lower class populations of São Luiz.

In the exercise of their profession, the *pagés* prepare beverages which are taken by their clients as purgatives or used for "bathing" to cure ills. These beverages consist of water in which leaves have been steeped. They are intended to free a person from his maladies, whether of a natural or supernatural character or to bring the client success in love, travel or business. *Curadores* also teach "prayers" which free their clients from natural and supernatural dangers and help them to fulfill their wishes. In addition to the "prayer" against the evil eye which was given above, the following which makes the individual invulnerable to all kinds of attack may be cited:

Meu corpo tem quatro cantos,	My body has four corners,
Cada canto tem un anjo	There is an angel in each;
Um é Sao Lucas, outro é Sao Mateus,	Saint Lucas in one, Saint Matthew in another
E o outro é o Senhor Deus	Our Lord in the other

Com todos os seus.	With all his saints.
Assim como Nosso Senhor	In the same manner that our
Jesus Cristo,	Lord Jesus Christ
Fechô o Santissimo Sacramento	Enclosed the Consecrated Host
no altá,	in the altar,
Assim ficará o meu corpo fechado	So my body will be invulnerable
Para todos os séculos, dos	Till the end of the centuries.
séculos, Amen.	Amen.

In addition to these activities, a *curador* may give consultation usually under possession by a spirit, generally conceived to the Indian. The spirit is then invoked. While under possession, the *curador* gives advice concerning business, or love, or pronounces cures. He also "makes passes" with his hands, thus fortifying his clients spiritually and physically and helping them to fulfill their desires.

Curadores are not, however, the only ones who prepare beverages, since the cult heads also engage in this kind of activity, also using leaves for preparing medicines. But their main activity, outside their functions as cult heads consists in petitioning the Catholic saints or the spirits whom they worship in favor of cult members or of clients. This is an activity only of a quasi magical character.

Some *curadores* engage in the *pagelança* dances of Indian origin, this being the outstanding activity which gives them their name. During the *pagelança* dances, which are held outside the city, the *pagé* is, as mentioned, possessed by an Indian spiritt. Under this state of possession he cures a client by taking from his body, as in the interior, a small object, a thorn, a needle, fish scales, or a small animal, often a lizard, placed in him by black magic. The dance in which these practitioners engage reproduces with very slight changes shamanistic dances among the autochtonous Indians. Such a dance has been described by Wagley for the Guajajara,[97] one of the tribes which apparently transmitted this shamanistic tradition to the city people through persons of mixed Indian-White or Indian-Negro descent who migrated to the city. Comparing Wagley's description with São Luiz practices, it becomes apparent that Indian ritual was borrowed in most details. For example, the Guajajara *pagé* smokes a cigar rolled of native tobacco with a covering of *tauari* leaf during the dance; in São Luiz, while the *pagé* during his dance smoked an ordinary commercial cigar, the name given to it is *tuari*. In São Luiz, as among the Guajajara, the dance of the *pagé* is accompanied by the rhythms of a small gourd rattle or *maracá*. With the Indians,

[97] Wagley, 1943, pp. 8-9. [Wagley now prefers to call the Guajajara by the more inclusive term Tenetehara. *Ed.*]

it is the *pagé's* assistant who plays the *maracá*, whereas, in São Luiz it is the *pagé* himself who plays the rattle, which is referred to as his "guide." As in the case of the city *pagé*, his Indian counterpart when possessed sucks out the object which is bringing harm to his client.

We may now indicate the various elements of non-Indian origin which can be observed in the *pagelança*. Elements of Catholic belief, for instance, have also been incorporated in the ceremony. The name of our Lady of Conception is invoked as the patroness of the dance in a song that is sung for her at its beginning:

Nossa Senhora de Conceição,	Lady of Conception,
Ora venha nos valer,	Mother of God,
Mae de Deus	Give us aid
Nesta ocasião.	At this time.

The room where the dance takes place is perfumed with incense to keep away evil spirits, especially the Devil. Like the cult groups, the *pagés* have sanctuaries in their houses with images of Catholic saints, and they as well as the persons who attend the *pagelança* are devout Catholics. In their minds, there is no inconsistency between the magic practices which they follow and Catholic beliefs.

In addition, some aspects of cult life have been incorporated in the *pagelança* dances, which may honor the spirits as well as invoke this power in healing. At a *pagelança* one can see persons under possession, and there are those who attend them especially for the experience of possession. Some of these are also members of the new Yoruban-derived cult houses, and it is said that they "own" one spirit in the cult line and another or several others in the *pagelança* line, while some spirits manifest themselves both in cult dances and in *pagelança* ceremonies.

Both these developments are recent, and indicate a growing integration of beliefs and practices of African, Indian and Catholic origin. Furthermore, this is being achieved despite the fact that the suspicions which have existed from the beginning between the *pagés* on the one hand and cult initiates on the other have continued. The *pagés* accuse the women cult members of being practitioners of black magic, while the latter often make the same accusation against the *pagés*.

These mutual accusations, in turn, reflect beliefs which are held by many Negroes and persons of mixed blood who do not participate either in the cult ceremonies or *pagé* dances. Yet, as *pagés* also cure, the flourishing of *pagelança* dances and other curative practices in which they engage seem mainly to be due to the fear of black magic which is shared by many people in this society.

Rural and urban comparisons. On comparing the richness of African religious survivals found in the city with their paucity in the rural areas, the foremost question in the mind of the student is how to explain the differences in this respect. This is no easy problem, and without detailed historical data on both acculturative situations, unfortunately lacking in this case, a definitive interpretation must await more information. It is known that the Dahomean and probably the Yoruban slaves who worked the plantations in the interior continued the worship of African deities, even though it was forbidden; and the slaves had to practice their religion in secret. A former slave, a man seventy-six years old, stated that the slaves used to have the dances for the *encantados* in the bush, far from the seat of the plantation. Furthermore, the number of slaves born in West Africa was probably very small in the rural region; mention of them is made, for instance, in the documents read in the town of Codó. These conditions, and the fact that the Negroes were indoctrinated with Catholicism indicate that the situation was not too favorable for the preservation in the country-side of the African religions.

In the city, the Dahomean and the Yoruban slaves were also taught Catholicism, but it seems that they had more freedom to preserve their aboriginal beliefs and to continue their religious traditions. The two cult houses which they established before the emancipation of slaves had freed slaves as their nuclei. When dances and ceremonies were held on the Saints' days, the Yoruban and the Dahomean slaves in the city were allowed to join their free "brothers."[98] Thus, unlike the plantation Negroes, no pressure was brought on these urban groups during slavery to give up their religious traditions. No official restrictions were imposed on these groups to discontinue their aboriginal religious beliefs and practices, and the fact that they managed to preserve their tribal identities may have worked in favor of the preservation of Dahomean and Yorubean religions. Furthermore, it must be mentioned that the Dahomean and Yorubean slaves introduced into Maranhão as well as in other parts of the New World brought with them religions that were so deeply set in Dahomean and Yorubean cultures that they represented one of the most highly institutionalized and best organized phases of these cultures. Other African religions—those of the peoples of Senegal and the Congo-Angola region—seem to have been less well-organized and

[98] This information was given by the eighty-year-old head of the Dahomean cult center.

more diffuse in structure. They thus had less chance of being continued than Yoruban and Dahomean beliefs and rituals, since traditions that are supported by strong institutionalized means are more resistant to change. This can be taken to explain why only few Congo-Angolan religious survivals[99], and none of Sengalese origin, are found in Maranhão, though it was from these regions that most of the Maranhão slaves came, the Dahomeans and the Yoruba, it will be recalled having been brought only in small numbers.

It is apparent that Dahomean beliefs have been maintained more strongly than Yoruban. In reference to this, informants stated that the Dahomeans and their descendants always formed a closed group. Today they are proud of their origin and of their religious traditions. They speak gratefully of the old Dahomean women who were so kind as to teach them everything about the "law," and of the latter's desire that they continue the worship of the *vodun*. In contrast, the urban group is less united, nor do strong ties bind them to their ancestors as in the case of the Dahomeans. Instead, the Yoruba in São Luiz complain that their ancestors did not teach them all that was to be learned about cult life since, as they phrased it, the "old women" did not wish to have their "fine religion" transmitted to "creoles" who would "spoil it." It is evident that these explanations help us to understand why the Yoruban group have lost so much of their religious traditions, while the Dahomeans have preserved theirs to a great degree. As we consider the greater unity and pride of the Dahomeans in comparison with the Yoruba, it becomes clear why initiates of the Yoruban group have gone away to establish their own centers, while none of the Dahomeans have ever split off from the original cult group.

In the Yoruban-derived cult houses, the Yoruban traditions are more modified by non-African elements than in the Yoruban cult center; the cult heads of these newer groups, lacking a knowledge of African traditions, can only transmit to their associates a segmented system of beliefs and of rituals. This helps us understand why the Yoruban-derived cult groups have engaged in the worship of Indian spirits while these spirits have not been accepted at all by the Dahomean groups and have only been accepted to a small extent by the Yoruba. Members of these two former groups are proud of their traditions and strive to transmit them to their descendants with a minimum of change. This is especially true of the Dahomeans, who believe that their own gods give them all the aid they require, and thus they feel no need for wor-

[99] Survivals of the religions of Congo-Angola peoples in Brazil are said to have been almost totally absorbed by those of Dahomean-Yoruban origin (Ramos, 1940, pp. 99-100, 111).

shipping Indian spirits. The members of the other cults, or persons who enter new cults, do not have such an integrated and satisfying conception of the supernatural powers as the Dahomean and the Yoruban groups; and are therefore more ready to adopt Indian spirits. That the *caboclo* deities play an important part in some of the Yoruban-derived houses is clearly indicated by the fact that the last of the three nights on which dances are held is the *caboclo* night: the Indian spirits in these houses thus have the important duty of closing the ceremonies. It should be said here in passing that some members of the Yoruban-derived cult houses show Indian physical traits.

It has been seen how in both rural community and city, Catholic and African-derived elements have mingled in the worship of the *encantados*. In the former, syncretization was found to have taken place mainly with reference to rites during the dances for the *encantados*. Identification between Catholic saints and African deities were not made but the latter, it must be remembered, had been almost totally forgotten. On the other hand, in all cult houses in the city sycretisms were found not only between Catholic and African elements of worship, but in the identification made between the Catholic saints and African deities. These syncretizations comprise an index of the integration that has been achieved between Catholic and African religious systems, a processs that is at present operative in the Yoruban-derived cult houses with reference to the adoption of Indian deities. As to the Catholic beliefs of these Negroes, no doubt remains that there has been a reinforcement of Catholic tendencies by reworking the corresponding features of African religion and by reinterpretation of Catholic beliefs in accordance with African patterns of worship.

An important difference that must be stressed between the rural and the urban districts concerns the degree of contact of these two negro groups with white persons. The isolation of the rural Negroes allows them to hold their dances entirely free from outside influences, while the city Negroes are aware that they belong to a larger society, to the white members of which their ceremonies appear as curious, if not obnoxious practices. This condition is especially true of the members of the two "orthodox" cult centers, but less so of the Yoruban-derived cult groups, whose houses, situated in the outskirts of the city, permit them to carry on their rites less conspicuously. Members of the two "orthodox" houses stated that in their opinion many people in São Luiz held their ceremonies in ridicule; and stated that others had accused them of practicing black magic. Cult initiates know also that the Church has taken a stand against the dances of their groups. This feeling tends to make the members of the Dahomean and the Yoruban center wary. In the Dahomean house, some ceremonies have been discontinued to avoid public criticism, ceremonies such as that in which the women, dressed in white, go to a public fountain to fill the water jars kept in the private room of their cult house, or the custom of tying a ribbon around the trunk of a large tree in the yard of the cult house, and leaving under it dishes containing food for the *vodun*. Women of the Yoruban cult center also admitted their fear of adverse opinion in a matter such as that of offering corn to Shapana on the streets during an epidemic.

A difference of some importance between the dances in the rural hinterland and in São Luiz lies in the fact that men and women participate as dancers in the rites of the interior, while in the city cult houses only women are allowed to dance. However, members of both "orthodox" centers stated that thirty or forty years ago some men also used to be possessed, though their number was small in comparison with that of the female dancers. But the police seem to have prohibited men from dancing; whatever the cause, older members of both houses will state that men are not allowed to dance since it is "immoral" for both men and women to participate in the same dance. Today, indeed, men would be criticized as effeminate if they danced, and even the practitioners of healing magic who usually dance are not free from this criticism. However, one man did continue to dance in several houses in the outskirts of the city until a few years ago.

Finally, an explanation drawn in economic terms, which takes into account the richness of ceremonialism in the city cult houses in contrast to the less impressive ceremonies in the country, should not be overlooked. Only in the city are the economic resources available for elaborate ceremonial clothes, for repairing or buying new drums, for sacrifices to the deities, and for ceremonies such as those of the *tambor de pagamento* in the two "orthodox" cult centers; and for an orchestra to play for a *ladainha* at the culut house. Thus, economic factors should be added to other historical conditions already mentioned in order to explain the difference in the extent of African religious survivals found in the city of São Luiz and in the rural areas of Maranhão.

CHAPTER SIX

THE SOUL, THE GUARDIAN ANGEL, AND THE RITES OF DEATH

Of all the four principal events in the life cycle of a Maranhão Negro—birth, adolescent, marriage and death—it is death that is outstandingly characterized in both the rural area and in the city of São Luiz by ceremonies of African origin. Thus while birth is marked by christening in the Church, adolescence by first communion, and marriage by the traditional Catholic rites, death is marked both by European rituals and by ceremonies that are a continuation of African customs. In addition, these ceremonies are given meaning by beliefs in the nature and destiny of the soul which can be partially traced to Africa; beliefs which, in reality, represent a fusion of European and African traditions of similar character, and which makes the rites they validate purposeful to the participants. As background for the description of these ceremonies among the Maranhão Negroes, then, we will first discuss their ideas as regards the soul and after life, and the related concept of the guardian angel.

Let us first consider the ideas of the rural Negroes. They believe that the soul and the guardian angel are the two spirits possessed by every human being. The soul is responsible for the person's everyday acts, while the guardian angel, "a sacred spirit," acts as the person's protector, and is constantly in his company until death. The soul gives life to the body, but at night, when a person sleeps, it may go far from the body. Rural Negroes state, therefore, that dreams represent the experiences which the soul has while the body sleeps, the places it visits and the activities in which it participates. During the absence of the soul, the guardian angel watches closely over the body; and then it is the angel that breathes, though breathing is held to be ordinarily a function of the soul.

A guardian angel may be weak or strong. It is strong only when its owner is diligent in saying the proper prayers in its honor: Ave Marias, Pater-Nosters and Salve Reginas. In addition, there is a special long prayer in which the protection of this being is evoked.

| Anjo da minha guarda | Angel, who watches over me, |
| Semelhança do Senhor, | Made in the image of Our Lord, |

Para mim fôste nascido
Para sê meu defensô.
Eu peço, anjo bendito,
Da vossa graça podê
Dos laços dos maldito
Pra Deus me defendê.
Tão guardado teja eu
E as minha compania,
Santíssimo Senho,
Nosso Anjo da Virgem Maria,
Com Deus eu me deito,
Com Deus eu me alevanto,
Com a graça de Deus,
Divino Espírito Santo.

For me you were born
To be my defender.
I beg you, blessed angel,
Bless me with your power,
Free me from demons
Defend me in the name of God.
Keep me safe
And those with me,
Very sacred Lord,
Angel of the Virgin Mary
With God I lie down,
With God I arise,
With the blessings of God
And of the blessed Holy Ghost.

A guardian angel "eats only prayers," the Negroes say, and it must be "fed" continuously to free its protégé from danger; for while it never abandons its protégé, it may be weakened if it does not receive the necessary "sustenance." And if a guardian angel becomes weak, anything may happen to the one it guards, since he is vulnerable both to natural and magical powers. Thus it is held that the soul with a weak guardian angel can be abducted by a sorcerer who may cause a person's death; and it is maintained that should a corpse perspire, this is a sign that the soul of the dead has been stolen by a sorcerer. In this way it is possible for a person to be buried without being really dead.

It is believed that the guardian angel casts a second shadow that can be seen when it is strong; and that, in addition to the shadow cast by a person's body and that of his guardian angel, one can also sometimes see the shadow of the soul. The shadow of the body is obviously the most dense, and that of the soul is said to be celarer than that of the guardian angel. When a man senses danger, he prays: "My body has warned me of something; O, my guardian angel, free me from this danger." The guardian angel is then believed to place himself both in front and in back of the man, thus protecting him from any danger.

The ideas held by the urban Negroes on the subject of the guardian angel are less elaborate than those of the rural group, but they have the same basic tenets of belief: that the guardian angel is a protecting spirit, that prayers strengthen it and that a person with a weak guardian angel can easily fall a victim to natural or supernatural forces; and that it never abandons a person to whom it belongs even if it has been weakened by neglect to offer prayers to it. The urban Negroes also believe as the rural folk do concerning the soul; that the spirit is responsible for a person's acts, that it enjoys the faculty of leaving the body at night, and that this is the reason why the person dreams.

Both urban and rural groups believe that when a man dies, the guardian angel goes to Heaven, while the destiny of the soul, determined by God, depends on the quality of its acts on earth, so that it may go to Heaven, to purgatory or to hell. If it does not go to Heaven, it may then appear to human beings when they are awake or in dreams: and a soul that does this —a "wandering" soul—is greatly feared. On the other hand, it is believed that the souls of the dead will help those who pray to them, and that they will intercede with God on behalf of human beings as do the saints. "Worship of souls is even better than worship of the saints," stated a member of the rural community, since these souls want to purify themselves and find salvation which can be facilitated if they receive prayers. In both city and country, "souls are interested in receiving Pater Nosters and masses."

The European form of the complex of ideas just described is only too obvious to need discussion. The concepts of the guardian angel, the destination of the soul, prayers, the help that souls can give those who pray to them— these are Catholic beliefs. However, some of the ideas held by the Maranhão Negroes concerning the guardian angel and the soul recall those held by the Africans from whom the Maranhão Negroes are derived. The Dahomeans and the Yoruba have the concept of multiple souls[1] which function as do the corresponding beings envisaged by the Negroes of Maranhão. The Bambara of the Senegal believe in a spirit that gives life to the body, and in another that goes away while the person is sleeping in a manner strikingly similar to that recorded above: "Le dya (double) jouit de la faculté d'abandonner le corps endormi pour aller vagabonder où bon lui semble et le spectacle de ses divagations, dont le corps le demeure témoins, constitue le rêve."[2] The peoples of the Angola-Congo region also believe in multiple souls.[3] Furthermore, a term such as to "feed" (*alimentar*) the guardian angel and the belief that the soul can be stolen by a sorcerer,[4] thus causing the person's death, are other characteristics which need only be mentioned to make clear their West African provenience. Finally, the attitudes of fear towards the soul of the dead on one hand, and respect and piety on the other, can best be interpreted as ideas which are derivative from both European and African concepts.[5]

Rites of death. Turning to describe the rites of death, we may now de-

[1] Herskovits, 1938, Vol. II, pp. 231-234; Farrow, 1926, pp. 130-132.
[2] Tauxier, 1927, p. 23.
[3] Peschuël-Loesche, 1907, pp. 299-302.
[4] Herskovits, 1938, Vol. I, p. 400; Tauxier, 1927, pp. 45-46.
[5] Herskovits, 1938, p. 198; Tauxier, 1927, pp. 29, 110.

scribe the funeral ceremonies of the rural area.[6] Soon after death has occurred, the news is transmitted from mouth to mouth, while messengers are sent to nearby communities to inform the inhabitants of the event. No work is done in the fields that day. On the reception of the news, work is stopped immediately—a custom that seems to have been observed since the days of slavery. "Our grandparents and great grandparents did the same in slave times," said one man, adding that a slave was usually sent to nearby plantations to notify the people on these plantations that "a black slave of my master has died," news which brought many slaves from other plantations for the burial.

In addition to the belief held today that work must be stopped in the fields because this is "the proper custom" (costume da terra), the Santo Antônio Negroes maintain that fear of the soul of the person who died also plays a part: that unless work is stopped, the soul of the dead will frighten those who continue working by throwing stones at them or by making strange noises, or even by causing a worker to injure himself. Even if no disturbance were experienced in the fields at the time of death, any untoward noises heard or any accidents occurring during the period of work or afterwards would be attributed to the soul. The implication of this is that the dead desires his funeral to be well attended, so that he will have a proper farewell, something that also seems to be reminiscent of the African attitude towards death in accordance with which only the person who has had a proper burial may expect admission into the land of the dead.[7]

In the house of the dead perosn, where relatives and close friends congregate as soon as they receive the news, Church prayers proper to the occasion have already been recited. The body is then washed by persons of the same sex as the deceased, and dressed in its best clothes; the body of a woman is dressed in a robe if this has been prepared previously by order of the deceased or of a member of her family. After being dressed, the body, hands crossed on the breast, is placed in an unslung hammock and laid out on some wooden boxes in the center of the principal room of the house. Two kerosene lamps are left burning, each a little above and to one side of the head of the deceased, while a statue of a Catholic saint, usually St. Mary, is placed on a wooden box at the head of the dead person. A heavy white cloth covers the body.

[6] This description is based upon observation made during the burial of an old woman, as well as on information obtained by interviewing.

[7] Herskovits, 1938, Vol. I, pp. 194, 400: Farrow, 1926, p. 108; Weeks, 1914, p. 266.

Several persons, generally women, keep watch, sitting on the floor on mats close to the walls. Other women are busy inside the house or in the back yard preparing food for those who attend the wake and the burial: relatives and friends from nearby communities, and friends and acquaintances of the village. A large quantity of rice is pounded and a pig is killed, for the visitors must be properly fed. If their is no pig to be killed, a friend will lend one; if rice is lacking, friends or relatives will willingly supply some. In addition, coffee and *cachaça*, a kind of rum, must be given to all who care for it. A few bottles of *cachaça* are bought at the village store by the family of the dead, while relatives who come from nearby villages generally bring more. The villagers hold it to be very important that food and *cachaça* be given in large amounts to those who come to attend the funeral, and this looms large as a mark of social prestige for the family of the dead person while, at the same time, it implies that a proper farewell is being given him.

The men congregate outside the house, where they talk and joke. Many of them show signs of having drunk large portions of *cachaça*. Larger amounts of this liquor are given to three or four men who are asked by a member of the family of the deceased to dig the grave where the body is to be buried, this being their compensation. The grave is made in the local cemetery, situated less than half a mile from the village on the road that leads to the town of Codó.

In the room where the deceased has been laid out, the women who keep watch over the body spend most of their time singing Church prayers called *benditos*.[8] These songs are prayers to God to permit the soul of the dead to be admitted into Heaven or, as the Negroes say following Catholic terminology, "to commend the soul of the deceased to God" (*encomendar a alma do defunto ao Senhor*). In the intervals between one song and another, comments are made on secular, even risqué, matters, and it is not unusual to hear persons laughing aloud, even relatives. If the watch over the body takes place during the night, *sentinela* is the term given to the wake.

Prayers are recited if the dead person was an adult. When an infant dies, prayers are not recited because it is necessary to pray God to let a "little angel" enter Heaven, since it has committed no sins, and thus has nothing for which to be forgiven. Instead of prayers, stories of kings and princesses or other tales of European origin, and animal tales derived from Africa, are told for amusement so that the hours of the wake for a dead child will not seem too long.

[8] For a description of similar customs in the interior of the state of Paraiba see Fernandes, 1938, pp. 65-74.

As the time for the burial draws near, some women in the group become possessed by their respective *encantados*. When possession comes on, they sing the songs sung during the ritualistic dances described in the chapter on religion, and make the guttural noises which usually accompany possession. As these women are now the spirits themselves, they may greet some of the persons present. One woman, possessed by a well-known and much respected *encantado,* Pedro Angaço, usually takes charge of the final arrangements for the burial. The white cloth that covers the body is withdrawn and the encantado comes near to it with a bowl containing water, in which several small branches of the sacred tree called *esturaque* have been steeped. With one of these he makes the sign of the cross over the body of the deceased sprinkling water over it, thus blessing the body in accordance with Church usage. Then the other *encantados* follow Pedro Angaço's example.

Now the closest relatives of the deceased, weeping and wailing, kneel and kiss the hands of the corpse, thus saying farewell to the dead person. Women and girls leave the room when the pall bearers enter carrying the long round pole which is inserted through the ends of the hammock. Three or four men at each end of it support this pole on their shoulders and take the body outside the house, where in the meanwhile a processsion has been organized by the woman possessed by Pedro Angaço. A girl in front of it carries the statue, usually of St. Mary, which was placed at the head of the deceased in the house; then a line of girls is formed behind the image bearer. Next come the adult women, and after these the men carrying the corpse. Behind the pall bearers, and at the side of the dead, is a group of men and women, both relatives and friends of the deceased.

As the procession starts towards the cemetery, the expression "brother of the souls" (*Irmao das Almas*) is continually shouted by men and women alike.[9] Some songs are also sung, songs for the *encantados* or songs of farewell to the dead. All the way to the cemetery, the shouts, "Brother of the souls," are accompanied by loud remarks and laughter, and a strong competition develops among the men to carry the body of the deceased. Reasons given for this competition were that "it is customary to do so," or that the dead is an inhabitant of the village and everybody wants to do him "a last favor." The real reason, however, would seem to be the belief that the soul will not appear to those who attend the funeral, and thus will not frighten them; and that it may even protect them. The competition to carry the body which develops among men who are for the most part under the influence of

[9] In Paraiba, the shouts *"Irmao das Almas"* serve to call people to come for the wake at the house of the deceased (Fernandes, 1938, pp. 64-65).

liquor may even result in a fight. One can see two men engaged in a bodily struggle, and if there is no outside intervention, the contenders may be seriously injured if knives or agricultural implements are handy.

When the procession arrives at the cemetery, the mourners circle the grave while two men descend into it to receive the body. Before it is lowered into the grave, however, *cachaça* is poured there, and the two men rub themselves with this liquor in order, as they say, to avoid the smell of the corpse. As the body is being handed down to the two men, the women surrounding the grave make the sign of the cross frequently and call out loudly "*Ai credo*," an expression that shows fear and piety. After it has been carefully put in place, the men with hoes, fill the grave with the earth piled at the sides, and every person participating in the burial throws a handful of earth on the grave. This is done as a symbol of farewell to the dead, and is also meant to prolong the permanence of the living on earth, since it is believed that by this means one will not meet the soul of the dead for a long time to come. The hammock is not buried. It is washed afterwards and continues to be used in the household. Of the personal belongings of the deceased, only his comb is buried with him.

After the grave has been filled with earth, a procession of the girls and women returns to the village singing the same songs they sung on their way to the cemetery. This procession disbands when it arrives in front of the village store. The men go back in small groups; most of them make their way to the river where they bathe. This has nothing to do with beliefs concerning the soul of the dead, however, but is rather to cleanse themselves after the exertions of carrying the corpse and filling the grave.

The burial of the deceased does not dissolve his ties with the living, since it is believed that his soul will haunt the house where he lived for the next seven nights after death, returning "to collect his sins" or "to take his track." As its return is feared by the living relatives, other persons may spend the first few nights there to keep the members of the household company.

On the seventh, fifteenth or thirthieth day after death takes place what is called the "visit of the grave" (*visita de cova*). The one observed in Santo Antônio took place on the seventh day. On this occasion, some of the relatives and friends of the dead meet and go to the cemetery where Church prayers are recited near the grave. Every five or six Ave Marias the women sing:

Amado Jesus, Joaquim,	Beloved Jesus, Joaquim,
Ana e José;	Anne and Joseph;

Eu dei meu coração	I gave my heart
Ao meu amado Jesus	To my beloved Jesus.

Beeswax candles made by the villagers are lighted and placed on the grave, and as each person places a candle he or she speaks to the body in the grave. In the case observed where the dead had been an old woman, participants said: "This is my candle, old woman;" "This was sent by Mary, old woman;" "I am lighting two candles for you, old woman," After saying their prayers they leave the cemetery and go to their homes. The soul is believed to offer thanks by protecting those who have lighted candles for them, and does not appear to frighten these persons.

Some visits to the grave are more elaborate than others. For instance, invitations are sometimes sent to relatives and friends of the neighboring villages. In such cases, food (rice and pork) and liquor and coffee are served to the visitors, and, if the deceased was an active member of the gorup that worships the *encantados*, a ritualistic dance is held at night, when it is believed the soul of the deceased may attend. However, the dance is no different from an ordinary dance for the *encantados*. In addition to periodical visits to the grave of a dead relative, a final formal "visit" may be made a year after death has occurred. This ends the series of obligations towards the soul of the dead.

We may now ask which of these mortuary rites or customs are African or show African features. There are few that do, and these few have been greatly modified in the rural setting. Of these, reference can be made, for instance, to the importance attached to providing food and drinks for the "mourners" and to the so-called "visit to the grave." The first occasion is reminiscent of the large expenditures made in West Africa on occasion of the burial of a relative,[10] while the institutionalized "visit to the grave" can be linked in the same way to the African custom of the definite burial.[11] Story-telling during the wake of a child is also an African pattern, though the substitution of Church prayers during the wake of an adult indicates that Catholic ways have supplanted the African. As we have seen, this is true of most of the complex described, but syncretization of African and European ways has been operative here as in the ceremonies of *encantado* worship. An outstanding example of syncretization in regards death ceremonies is provided by the intervention of the African-like spirits, the *en-*

---

[10] Herskovits, 1938, Vol. I, Chaps. XIX and XX; Farrow, 1926, p. 108; Talbot, 1926, Vol. III, p. 469.

[11] Herskovits, 1938, Vol. I, Chaps. XIX and XX.

cantados, in the funeral. Finally, the attitudes towards the soul of a recently dead person: fear, on one hand, respect and "worship" on the other, can be incorporated into the system of ideas about the soul which represents, as we have seen, a fusion of African and European patterns.

Urban rites. Mortuary rites among city Negroes are essentially the same as those followed by Whites in São Luiz and, in general, by urban Brazilians everywhere, but the great importance attached by the Negroes to being properly buried is a trait of psychology that can best be interpreted as a characteristic derived from West Africa. For Africans, only he who is properly buried can enter the land of the dead and assume his rightful place there, which means that the living are greatly concerned with the manner in which they will be buried.[12] This attitude among the Maranhão Negroes takes the form of anxiety that they should have a proper funeral, something that is foremost in their minds.

The concept of a proper burial focuses on the kind of coffin in which a person will be buried. In conversation with Negroes of both sexes, one often hears how abhorrent is the idea that they may be buried in a "bare coffin" (that is, one which is unadorned) because they lack the funds to buy a better one or because the burial has to be made at the City Government's expense. People told how others would make derogatory remarks about such a coffin, and it is this dread that drives so many São Luiz Negroes to become members of a burial association existing in the city, the object of which is to provide proper funerals for their associates, who pay monthly dues.

To indicate the importance of the funeral to São Luiz Negroes, we may best turn to a description of burial customs there. After the body of the dead person has been washed, it is placed in the main room of the house, in a coffin, ordinarily made of wood, painted on the outside and decorated with black or purple ribbons. If the deceased is a man, he is dressed in his best clothes, preferably a dark suit, while a woman is dressed in a shroud in most cases meant to represent one of the manifestations of Our Lady. Lighted candles are placed at the four corners of the coffin, and one or more statues of the saints are put at the head of the coffin. On chairs or benches, close to the walls of the room, sit the persons who have come to pay their respects to the dead and to his family.

When the body remains overnight in the house, as is ordinarily the case,[13] those who spend the night or part of it there are said, as in the interior, to

[12] Herskovits, 1941, p. 198; Weeks, 1914, p. 266.
[13] By city ordinances a burial has to take place within twenty-four hours after death.

have come for the wake (*sentinela*). During the *sentinela* some customs can be observed which do not occur in white houses, customs of African derivation are designed to entertain the mourners so that the hours of watching will be shortened: refreshments are served, stories are told, and riddles are recited. The stories are mostly of the type called "of kings and queens;" they are Afro-European tales in which a king or a prince has many adventures at the end of which he marries a princess who has, perhaps, been bewitched. Other stories are those to be read in popular magazines. No animal tales seem to be known. The riddles are a very popular form of amusement. The following is quite well known:

| Campo grande, gado miudo, | A large open space, short cattle, |
| Moça bonita e homem carrancudo. | A pretty girl and a sour-looking man. |

A large open space stands for sky; short cattle for stars; a pretty girl for the moon and a sour-looking man for the sun. Another riddle goes:

Quatro pé em cima de quatro pé;	Four feet on four feet;
Esperando qatru pé;	Waiting for four feet;
Quatro pé não veio;	Four feet did not come;
Quatro pé foi embora; ficô quatro pé.	Four feet went away; four feet remained.

The answer is a cat on a table waiting for a rat that did not come; the cat went away and the table remained in its place.

Cards or other games are also played at wakes. One very popular game dramatizes a proposal. Some women, generally unmarried ones, stand near the coffin, and a couple who represent their father and mother seat themselves on chairs close to each other. In the next room, or outside the house, there are some men. At the start of the game, one of the latter knocks at the door, which is closed, and the "father" tells another man who represents a butler to see who it is. The butler opens the door and comes back after talking to the visitor, and tells his "master:" "It is a citizen who wants to talk to you." The visitor is invited to enter the room to talk to the "father" of the girls. After being asked what he wants, he replies in the following manner: "I understand that you have some daughters of marriageable age, and I came to propose to one of them." The chief of the family asks the candidate his profession, and he answers. He is then told to talk to the "mother" of the girls, because her consent is necessary. She consents to the "match" and tells the young man to choose the girl he wants to "get married to." This he does and extends his hand toward her. If the girl accepts the proposal she gives him her hand and he stands then at her side. If she refuses she turns her face away and the young man leaves the room. This, however, rarely occurs, because the girl who thus refuses is censured and eliminated from the game. The game is repeated until all girls have been "married."

Another form of diversion is the "soldier game." All those in the room surround the coffin and each is given a military rank ranging from private to general. The general starts the game saying that somebody is missing: "I review my battalion and the sergeant is missing." The person whose rank is called answers: "The sergeant is not missing, but the first lieutenant (or someone else) is." The latter must then answer that he is not missing but someone else is. If the answer does not come immediately, or if there is any mistake, the person who has failed to answer correctly must exchange rank with the person who queried him.

Aside from these customs, which are reminiscent of the festivities to amuse and honor the dead in Africa,[14] all others connected with death conform to Brazilian practice. This is true, for instance, of the procession to the cemetery, as well as of the burial itself. The coffin is carried by hand when it is taken out of the house, and is generally taken to the cemetery in a hearse. A priest will be paid to accompany the procession and will recite Catholic prayers at the cemetery near the grave while the body is being lowered into it and for a short time afterwards. It is customary, as in the interior, to throw a handful of earth on the grave as a symbol of farewell to the dead. The house of the dead is cleaned after the body leaves, and the front door and all windows are customarily closed for a week, until the mass said on the seventh day, and relatives and friends often come and spend nights in the house of the dead in the company of the bereaved relatives. Before going to bed those in the house may pray that the soul of the dead rest in peace.

Cult rites. We may now turn to a description of the ceremonies held in the houses of worship of the *encantados* when a cult initiate or one of the musicians or a player of the iron gong dies. The name *tambor de choro* is given in all cult centers to these rites.

When a cult initiate falls ill, it is customary to bring her to her house of worship for treatment. The reasons for this are that the invalid will be in closer contact with the deity she worships as well as the other deities of the cult house who can give her supernatural help. There is also a practical aspect to the matter, since the patient is nursed by the other cult initiates who attend to her needs carefully. Should death ensue, the body is washed by the surviving cult initiates, and dressed in the white regalia of its god; over this dress is worn a shroud representing one of the manifestations of

[14] Herskovits, 1938, Vol. I, Chaps. XIX and XX; Farrow, 1926, pp. 107-108; Weeks, 1914, pp. 269, 275.

Our Lady, Our Lady of the Rosary, Our Lady of Loudres, Our Lady of Conception, and so forth.

In the Dahomean house, the regalia of the *vodun* worshipped by the deceased are kept by the cult head, to be worn by the woman who next becomes possessed by that *vodun*. The coffin is placed in an inside room, close to the veranda where the dances for the *vodun* are usually held, and the persons who attend the burial sit on chairs or benches. A large basin is placed on the floor of the dancing space. It contains a mixture of water, wine and *cachaça*, with sand at the bottom, and the *vodunsi* dressed in white garb sit on chairs or stools and take their places around it. A half calabash is placed upside down in the center of the basin and the *vodunsi*, who hold wooden sticks, beat the rhythms of the funeral songs on the borders of the basin and on the calabash. These songs are in Fō:

> Okaje okae madayo
> Ayo simena fiho
> O file majokae
> O kamarado nue madayo
> Ayo simena siho.

> Ohi ohunailo
> Ohi ohunailo
> Dada miho nakokue
> Obolo hunjeleto.

Members of the Dahomean cult center state that the purpose of these songs is to bid farewell to their "sister" and tell her how sad they are that she has had to leave them. The atmosphere in which this rite is carried on is sad, often the women weep.

In the corner of the dancing space, the drummers play their drums, the small and the middle-sized ones are played if the cult initiate was a *vodunsi-ahe,* or if the deceased is a drummer who has never played the *hun,* the big drum. For this instrument is played only if the dead was a *vodunsi-hanjai,* or a drummer who usually played it at dances. In addition to the drums, two pots are also played at death rites. These are beaten with a strip of stiff leather. Before the end of the ritual, the two pots as well as the calabash must be broken. The name *zēli* which is given in Dahomey to the funerary drum[15] is applied by the Dahomean group in Maranhão to designate the beat of the drums on this occasion, and is by extension applied to the entire ceremony. Members of the house, friends, and visitors drop coins in the basin, this being what is called a "precept" demanded by the beliefs

[15] Herskovits, 1938, Vol. I, p. 363.

held of the cult center. The money is used for expenses connected with the masses later read in the Catholic Church for the soul of the dead.

If the ceremonial above described cannot be held when a *vodunsi* dies, either because the death of the *vodunsi* occurs during Lent when no ceremonies can be held at the cult house or because, for instance, it has been impossible to carry the drums to the house of the deceased (in the event she has died at her own house), a ceremony of the same type is held later, six months or a year after the day of the death. It then receives the name *sihun.*

The funeral procession and burial rites follow the pattern already described. The following elements, however, make the death ritual of a cult member different from that of an ordinary person. On returning from the cemetery, every member of the cult house must wash his hands, wrists, and head with the holy water called *amasin*. This is done at the entrance of the cult house, where a gourd with *amasin* has been left for this purpose. When all are cleansed, what remains is thrown in the street. This rite is believed to absolve the cult members from any further contacts with the dead. The other rite that is observed in the Dahomean house is held after the mass of the seventh day, when those who return from Church have a ceremonial meal at the cult house, which includes the African dish *cariru*[16] prepared especially for this occasion.

In the Yoruban house, the dead cult initiate is dressed in the same manner as in the Dahomean cult center, but in her coffin a rosary and her ritual bracelets are placed underneath the pillow on which the head rests. The body is placed in the room close to the dancing space, and the cult initiates, dressed in white as in the Dahomean house, sit on mats on the floor. The drummers are in their customary places and as they begin to play, the cult initiates sing the *Imbarabo* song, followed by songs of the Naga, the Tapa and the *caboclo* lines, and omitting only the songs of the *encantado* of the deceased. This ceremony lasts three or four hours, and ends as the cult initiates get up and walk and dance about the coffin, singing, each in turn blessing the body with holy water. It may be noted in passing that if this ceremony cannot for any reason be held at the proper time, there is no provision for it to be held later on. After returning from the cemetery, the cult initiates wash their heads and hands, and sprinkle their feet with *amasin,* which, in the manner described, is thrown outside the door to sever all connections between the living and the dead. For seven nights, just as in the Dahomean cult house, the initiates recite a series of

[16] See above p. 99.

Church prayers for the soul of the dead. All cult initiates then sleep on mats on the floor of the veranda. On the seventh day of the death, the initiates attend mass for the soul of the deceased, returning to the cult house afterwards where the African dish *amala,* that is *cariru* and *acaraje,*[17] is ceremonially eaten.

Some time before midnight on the seventh night a final rite is held. This consists in disposing of some of the paraphernalia used by the deceased as a member of the cult house. Two of the cult initiates and a drummer in a canoe, take to the sea a white cloth, sandals and a portion of the *amala* which was given the cult initiates after the mass. These things form what is called *carga*;[18] they are placed inside a basket which is set down on the water from whence it is thought to be taken by the soul of the deceased. If this ritual is not properly performed, the soul will remain to haunt the cult house or the homes of the cult initiates and cause them to have evil dreams. In this event, the ceremony would have to be held again; but this has never been necessary in the Yoruban cult center.

In the Yoruban-derived cult houses, the *tambor de choro* may be given twice, once on the day of the funeral and again some six months later, or only once, after burial has already taken place. The deceased is dressed as in the two orthodox houses. Some of her ceremonial regalia are placed with her in the coffin. Upon the return from the cemetery, the cult initiates wash their hands and face in sacred water called *veveu.* For seven nights they meet at the cult house where they pray for the soul of the dead, and on the night of the last day of the prayers, the *carga* is taken to the sea. The *tambor de choro* itself copies that held at the Yoruban center, but the body is placed in the middle of the dancing space. The cult initiates dressed in white sit on mats on the floor surrounding the coffin, rubbing their hands and singing in low voices.

Six months later, a new ceremony is held to end mourning. At this time, the cult initiates sit on benches close to the walls in the dancing space; they are dressed in white. The drummers play on two drums which are covered by elaborate white cloths; an iron gong and a rattle are also played. The beats of the drums and of the gong are soft and the cult initiates sing in low voices. Their heads are bowed, and the faces of all show sadness. The songs are those for all the *encantados* worshipped by the cult group.

[17] See above p. 99.

[18] A similar custom is found among the members of Bahian and Porto Alegre cult houses. There the name *carrega* is used instead of *cargo.* (Herskovits, 1943, pp. 507-508).

The center of the dancing space is kept free and no one is allowed to cross it, since it is believed that the souls of deceased members of the cult center are dancing there.

At seven o'clock, an hour before one such ceremony ended, some of the cult initiates went to the room which contained the sanctuary with images of saints, that of St. Barbara in the middle. Here a *ladainha* was said to honor St. Barbara and other saints, and the soul of the deceased cult initiate. The cult initiates then returned to the dancing space, where the *tambor de choro* continued for a short time. Then, one of the ranking cult initiates came in the room and "disinfected" the dancing space. She went inside the house in the private room and returned with a bowl of holy water which she sprinkled around the dancing space, through the veranda, along the corridor le   to the street, finally throwing the remainder into the street by the entrance door. This was done to cause the souls of the dead to depart. While the water was being sprinkled, the cult initiates stood in a semi-circle; the members of the audience were urged to stand up. After this, a song was sung aloud and the instruments were played in the ordinary manner. As the song ended, the participants returned to their seats and at a sign from the "guide," the second ranking person of the cult group, all left the room quietly and slowly, in line. This ended the ceremony for the soul of the dead, the last song signifying that an ordinary rite could thereafter be held. An hour later, after *cariru* and coffee had been served to house members and guests, a dance for the *encantados* began. This is called *tambor de limpeza,* that is, it is designed to cleanse the cult house from any presence of death.

In addition to these ceremonies, an annual *"cariru"* is generally prepared and served in most of the city's cult houses in honor of the souls of the dead. This ceremony takes place on All Soul's Day, November first.[19]

It is thus apparent that retentions of African mortuary rites in São Luiz are to be noted chiefly in the cult houses where the worship of African and the African-like deities has persisted. The patterns followed in all of these houses tend to be the same, although differences in detail are to be noted. The paraphernalia of the dead cult initiates is not sent to sea in the Dahomean cult house, as is the case in the Yoruban cult houses, but the rites of farewell to the deceased celebrated by the Dahomeans are more African than those held at the Yoruban or the Yoruban-derived centers. Compared to the ceremonies held for the dead in the interior, those

[19] In many Catholic countries All Souls' Day is November second but custom varies in Brazil and some other areas.

in the city cult houses are markedly closer to the African pattern. And as regards the Negro population of São Luiz as a whole, it can be said that the general attitude of both members and non-members of the cult houses towards proper burial, as well as the presence of games and other forms of amusement during wakes, are reminiscent of African mortuary practices. The ideas of the Negroes about the relationship between dead and living, especially those who are cult members—ideas originally African, now merged with similar European beliefs—indicate that the mortuary rites hold for them psychological and functional, as well as formal meaning. As in the interior, there has been syncretization of beliefs and of ceremonies, Roman Catholic and African-derived elements, that now form a unified system of belief and ritual.

CHAPTER SEVEN

RESUMÉ OF MARANHAO NEGRO ACCULTURATION

The Negroes of the rural and the urban communities in the state of Maranhão in northeastern Brazil, studied in the course of the research on which this account of their lives has been based, have made a successful adaptation to the acculturative situation into which they were plunged in this New World setting. They preserved many African patterns, accepted many traits of the European culture of the masters, borrowed from the indigenous Indians and combined all into a new body of custom that is a going concern. In the economic sphere, while they have preserved the African traditions of cooperative work, and the economic independence of the women, they also successfully participate in the Western economic system. In the realm of family organization, they have translated their aboriginal polygynous patterns into one of successive unions, thus making a workable accomodation to the monogamous tradition. In religion, they have maintained African or African-like beliefs and practices syncretizing them with the many Catholic beliefs and rites they have adopted and reinterpreted.

It should be stressed that the Negroes of Maranhão have an integrated culture; that they are unaware of any conflict between the aspects of their culture that are of African and European derivation. In this respect, they differ markedly from the Negroes of Haiti, whose psychological atmosphere, characterized by "instability of attitude and emotional expression" in the words of Herskovits, is that or "socialized ambivalence."[1] The rural Negroes of Maranhão, certainly live their lives under no such conflict, although as might be expected, the urban Negroes do experience some tensions, partly because they live in an environment where more problems have to be met in any case, and partly because they are in closer contact with Whites whose moral and religious patterns differ in certain respects from their own. These insecurities are shown by the greater fear of black magic in the city as compared to the rural group. But *pagelança* practices and other forms of curative and preventive magic have, in this connection, the important function

[1] Herskovits, 1937, pp. 295-296.

of annulling such fears, so that the urban Negroes are to be regarded as having developed their own means for emotional security, though these are admittedly not as effective as the adjustments of the rural community.

The results of the acculturative process are thus, in general, the same among both groups, though differences in degree of acculturation can be observed as we pass from one to the other. For though it cannot be said that either group is more acculturated to European ways of life than the other, it is evident that the rural community emphasizes such African patterns as cooperative work, the economic independence of the women, and successive common-law unions to a much great extent than the urban; while the urban setting has been more conducive to the survival of African religious practices.

This "differential acculturation" reflects specific differences in the histories of the two communities. Indeed, the value of the historical type of explanation of cultural phenomena emerges strikingly in a study such as this, where the multiple factors with whose integration an historical analysis is concerned can themselves be explained only through reference to concrete historical facts.

Thus the African tradition of cooperative work was continued by the patterns of gang labor under slavery. After the liberation of the slaves, when the Negroes came to own land, this tradition found expression in the practice of labor exchange. In the city, however, wage labor eliminated most opportunities for cooperative work. Or to take a second instance, it is apparent that the African tradition of the independent economic position of women was not lost during slavery, since women did a large part of the work in the fields, and thus, even as slaves, maintained relative equality with the men. Since liberation they have continued to do this kind of labor, a practice which is not discouraged by the men who are quick to acknowledge the value of their contribution. The relative independence resulting from this has given them a place of semi-autonomy in family life. Since the urban women do not have this type of economic outlet, those in the country wield more economic power than their city sisters.

African polygynous patterns were suppressed during slave times, but, on the other hand, the Negroes did not practice monogamy. Unions seem to have been weak, and the pattern of successive unions of the *amigação* type could be easily laid down. This was, indeed, to the advantage of the white masters, in whose economic interest it was to produce slave children. After slavery, the custom of successive common-law unions continued, especially where isolation protected the Negroes from exposure to white patterns of morality. In this way, the African polygynous tradition was translated into a new form which was acceptable in the time of slavery to Whites and Negroes alike. Today, however, the city Negroes are conscious of white criticism of their *amigação* unions. That there are cases in which the need is felt to employ magic to steal the affection of one of the partners to such a union, is perhaps an indication that adaptation to successive monogamy is less successful in the city than in the village. Multiple unions also thrive better in the rural area than in the city, a fact which seems to give further indication that conditions there have been more favorable to the maintenance of African-like family patterns than those in an urban setting.

In the sphere of religion, however, we find the situation reversed, at least when consideration is given to Africanisms of Dahomean-Yoruban provenience, since it was established that the religious practices of certain groups of city Negroes are far closer to West Africa conditions, than are those of the people in the country. Some historical data at our disposal shed light on the differences that were found between the two groups, though these data are insufficient to afford any final explanation. Insofar as can be established, African religious ceremonies in the rural areas were suppressed by the slave-owners. In the city, on the other hand, the Dahomean and the Yoruban cult groups were able to continue their practices, since there were enough freed Negroes to establish cult centers. These groups were united moreover, and proud of their African traditions, which they strove in every way to preserve.

In contrast to the preservation of Dahomean and Yoruban religious beliefs and practices in São Luiz, few that derive from the Angola-Congo region of Africa are found, while none whatsoever of Senegalese origin exist in recognizable form, either in the country or in the city. This is to be explained to a considerable extent by the fact that in Africa the cults of these later peoples are more loosely organized and, therefore, could offer less resistance to attack than the closely organized Dahomean and Yoruban groups. Thus, it was that the Dahomean and the Yoruban beliefs and ceremonies were, and continue to be, disseminated in São Luiz.

The appearance of a new cult house, although it would appear to be due to both historical and psychological causes, cannot, however, be simply explained. It would be essential at the very least to make a detailed study of the reasons why people join these new centers of worship, a question which could only be touched on during the period of this research. It is apparent, however, that the newest centers are adopting elements of European and Indian origin as well as the African rites, and that these are being integrated with beliefs and practices of African derivation, a process which is being facilitated by similarities in the supernatural beings and forms of worship common to all.

Other African beliefs that have been preserved by the Negroes of Maranhão are those concerning multiple souls, and the belief in magic. This has been achieved by reinterpreting European beliefs in terms of aboriginal African patterns, or by merging the two. The special form taken by the belief in the soul and the guardian angel are an example of how those processes eventuated while, in the case of magical beliefs—excluding those which are clearly of Indian origin—we also see both African and European inspiration. In addition, it was shown how the worship of the Catholic saints, especially in the village, has been endowed with characteristics which can be clearly traced to Africa, the concept of these beings as an intimate part of everyday life, and the contractual nature of the relations between man and the saints being cases in point. It should be stresssed, however, that the kind of Catholicism that Africans met with in Maranhão facilitated this processs, since the saints were treated by the Portuguese, and are today regarded by a considerable number of their descendants in Brazil, as beings that have full participation in current happenings.

It was shown, also, how African and Catholic belief and ritual were syncretized in relation to death and burial, death beeing the only one of the four main events in the life cycle of an individual that is surrounded by retentions of African custom. The greater purity of African type in the cult centers of São Luiz, when compared with the forms they take in the rural districts, is further indication that these centers of worship preserved Dahomean and Yoruban beliefs and rituals more systematically than anywhere else in the area considered in this study.

In this enumeration of what happened to African customs in Maranhão and of the establishment of the present culture, we see clearly the work of certain processes the operation of which is by no means confined to this region. In utilizing the convention of successive unions to adapt polygynous forms to a monogamic pattern, we see at work the process of *reinterpretation* which, as just indicated, also operated in regard to religion, as, for instance, in the interior where the *encantados* are charatcerized as "angels" of the Church. It has also been seen how this process operated so that similar traditions often reinforced each other, or merged into a new form that combined elements of the ones from which the new form was derived, this being in accordance with a related assumption which guided this work: the assumption of the *One World cultural province* that provides underlying similarities to European and African customs which, on the surface, seem dissimilar.

Syncretization, another process, was seen to have been most extensive among cult groups in the city, where, as elsewhere in the New World, African gods are identified with saints of the Church, while, in addition, ceremonies of the Church and of African origin are held on the same occasion, and to the same ends.

A final hypothesis that was put to the test by this study was that every culture has a focal area which comprises an aspect of it that is one of the most, if not the most resistant to change under contact. The materials presented on religious life, wherein lies the focus of African cultures, have shown that this hypothesis has validity when applied to the two societies studied here. For even where African religious beliefs or practices have been greatly diluted, as in the interior or as among most of the city people, religion continues to be the main validating force of life, to which people cling for both "intellectual" and emotional reasons, that is, both to explain life and the universe, and to help them in the solution of life's problems. The preservation of religion as a focus of these Negro cultures has of course been facilitated by the fact that their ancestors found in Brazil a culture which laid great stress on this particular aspect of life, a stress which has not been challenged in São Luiz or in Santo Antônio. Nonetheless, the fact that so much of the religion of Africa survived in this setting, shows how here, as elsewhere in the New World, this principal concern of the aboriginal culture of the Negroes was the outstanding aspect of African cultures to resist the pressure of the dominant culture under the handicaps to retention set by slavery.

BIBLIOGRAPHY

AMARAL, BRAZ H. DO
  1927. "Os grandes mercados de escravos africanos—As tribus importadas—Sua distribuição regional." *Revista do Instituto Historico e Geographico Brasileiro*, Tomo especial, Vol. 5, pp. 435-496.
BASCOM, WILLIAM R.
  1941. "Acculteration among Gullah Negroes." *American Anthropologist*, Vol. 43, pp. 43-50.
  1944. "The Sociological Role of the Yoruba Cult Group," *American Anthropological Association, Memoir Series*, No. 46.
BECKWITH, MARTHA
  1929. *Black Roadways, a Study in Jamaican Folk Life*. Chapel Hill.
CALOGERAS, JOAO P.
  1927. "A politica exterior do imperio—as origens." *Revista do Instituto Historico e Geographico Brasileiro*, Tomo especial, pp. 1-471.
  1938. *Formacao historica do Brasil*. 3d ed., Sao Paulo.
CARNEIRO, EDISON
  1936. *Religiões Negras*. Rio de Janeiro.
CARVALHO, H. A. DIAS DE
  1890. *Ethnographica e Historia Tradicional dos povos da Lunda*. Lisboa.
CHATELAIN, HELI
  1894. "Folk-Tales of Angola." *Memoirs of the American Folk-Lore Society*, No. 1.
DELAFOSSE, MAURICE
  1931. *Negroes of Africa*. Washington.
DORSAINVIL, J. C.
  1931. *Vodun et Nevrose*. Port-au-Prince.
FARROW, STEPHEN S.
  1926. *Faith, Fancies and Fetich, or Yoruba Paganism*. London.
FERNANDES, CONCALVES
  1937. *Xangôs do Nordeste*. Rio de Janeiro.
  1938. *O Folclore magico do Nordeste*. Rio de Janeiro.
FRAZIER, E. F.
  1939. *The Negro Family in the United States*. Chicago.
  1942. "The Negro in Bahia, Brazil: A Problem in Method." *American Sociological Review*, Vol. 7, pp. 465-478.
FREYRE, GILBERTO
  1936. *Casa-Grande & Senzala*, 2nd ed., Rio de Janeiro.
HALLOWELL, A. I.
  1945. "Sociopsychological Aspects of Acculturation." *In* Ralph Linton (ed.), *The Science of Man in the World Crisis*. New York, pp. 171-200.

129

HAMBLEY, WILFRED D.
1934. "The Ovimbundu of Angola." Field Museum of Natural History, *Anthropological Series, Publication* 329.

HERSKOVITS, MELVILLE J.
1937 *a. Life in a Haitian Valley.* New York.
1937 *b.* "African Gods and Catholic Saints in New World Negro Belief." *American Anthropologist,* Vol. 39, pp. 635-643.
1938. *Dahomey.* 2 Vols., New York.
1941. *The Myth of the Negro Past.* New York.
1943 *a.* "The Southernmost Outposts of New World Africanisms." *American Anthropologist,* Vol. 45, pp. 495-510.
1943 *b.* "The Negro in Bahia, Brazil: A Problem in Method." *American Sociological Review,* Vol. 8, pp. 394-402.
1944. "Drums and Drummers in Afro-Brazilian Cult Life." *The Musical Quarterly,* Vol. 30, pp. 477-492.
1945. "The Processes of Cultural Change." *In* Ralph Linton (ed.), *The Science of Man in the World Crisis,* New York, pp. 143-170.

HERSKOVITS, M. J. and F. S.
1937. "Suriname Folk-Lore." *Columbia University Contributions to Anthropology,* Vol. 27.
1943. "The Negroes of Brazil." *Yale Review,* Vol. 32, pp. 263-279.

JOHNSON, CHARLES S.
1934. *Shadow of the Plantation.* Chicago.

JOHNSON, (REV.) SAMUEL
1921. *The History of the Yorubas, from the Earliest Times to the Beginning of the Protectorate.* London.

LACHATANERE, ROMULO
1942. *Manual de Santeria.* Habana.

LANDES, RUTH
1940. "Fetish Worship in Brazil." *The Journal of American Folk-Lore,* Vol. 53, pp. 261-270.

LE HERISSÉ, A.
1911. *L'Ancien Royaume du Dahomey.* Paris.

MAGALHAES, J. V. COUTO DE
1876. *O Selvagem.* Rio de Janeiro.

MARQUES, A. CESAR
1870. *Diccionario Historico-Geographico do Maranhão.* Maranhão.

MELO FRANCO, A. A. DE
1944. *Desenvolvimento da Civilização Material do Brasil.* Rio de Janeiro.

MORAES FILHO, NELLO
1901. *Festas e Tradições Populares do Brasil.* Rio de Janeiro.

NADEL, S. F.
1942. *A Black Byzantium.* London.

ORTIZ, FERNANDO
1917. *Los Negros Brujos.* Madrid.

PECHUEL-LOESCHE, E.
1907. *Volkskunde von Loango.* Stuttgart.

PIERSON, DONALD
1942. *Negroes in Brazil.* Chicago.
POWDERMAKER, HORTENSE
1939. *After Freedom.* New York.
PRADO JUNIOR, CAIO
1942. *Formação Histórica do Brasil Contemporâneo.* São Paulo.
PRICE-MARS, L.
1928. *Ainsi Parla L'Oncle.* Port-au-Prince.
RAMOS, ARTHUR
1935. *O Folk-Lore Negro do Brasil.* Rio de Janeiro.
1940. *O Negro Brasileiro.* 2nd ed., Rio de Janeiro.
1943. *Introdução a Antropologia Brasileira.* I, Rio de Janeiro.
Second volume in preparation.
REDFIELD, R., LINTON, R., and HERSKOVITS, M. J.
1936. "Memorandum for the Study of Acculturation." *American Anthropologist,* Vol. 38, pp. 149-152.
REUTER, E. B.
1938. *The American Race Problem.* 2nd ed., New York.
RIBEIRO, RENE
1945. "On The *Amaziado* Relationship, And Other Aspects Of The Family In Recife (Brazil)." *American Sociological Review,* Vol. 10, pp. 44-51.
RODRIGUES, NINA
1932. *Os Africanos no Brasil.* São Paulo.
SIMONSEN, ROBERTO C.
1937. *Historia economica do Brasil,* II. 2 vols., São Paulo.
SIMPSON, GEORGE E.
1945. "The Belief System of Haitian Vodun." *American Anthropologist,* Vol. 47, pp. 35-39.
TALBOT, P. A.
1926. *The Peoples of Southern Nigeria,* II and III. 4 vols., London.
TAUXIER, LOUIS
1937. *Moeurs et Histoire des Peuls.* Paris.
WAGLEY, CHARLES
1943. "Notas sobre Aculturação Entre Os Guajajara."
Boletin do Museu Nacional, No. 2, pp. 1-12.
n.d.   *Tenetehara of Brazil.* (manuscript).
WEEKS, JOHN H.
1914. *Among the Primitive Bakongo.* London.